A Visitor's

to Dealey Plaza

National Historic

Landmark

Including

©1995 Conover Hunt
ISBN–0–9648131–0–6

Published by
    The Sixth Floor Museum
    411 Elm Street
    Dallas, Texas 75202-3301
    214 653-6666

All rights reserved. No part of this book may be reproduced in any form without written permission from the publisher.

Printed in the United States of America by Dynagraphics, Inc., Dallas, Texas

Design by Tom Dawson Graphic Design

COVER ILLUSTRATION:
The president and first lady riding in the motorcade on Main Street in downtown Dallas.
Walt Sisco, courtesy The Dallas Morning News

A Visitor's Guide to Dealey Plaza National Historic Landmark

DALLAS, TEXAS

by

CONOVER HUNT

Published by

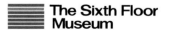
The Sixth Floor Museum

A small selection of the many books written about the Kennedy assassination.

Andy Reisberg, courtesy Mary Ferrell

Table of Contents

Introduction

*The past is what you remember,
imagine you remember,
convince yourself you remember,
or pretend to remember.*
•
HAROLD PINTER

by

J E F F   W E S T
*Executive Director,
The Sixth Floor Museum*

SACRED GROUND

In our country we preserve the places where our heroes have fallen—the Alamo, Gettysburg, the USS Arizona. We take the sites of tragedy and bloodshed and consecrate them through preservation, interpretation and commemoration.

We do these things to help us *remember.*

On November 22, 1963, Dealey Plaza became forever etched in our country's collective memory when President John F. Kennedy was assassinated. In the intervening years literally millions of people from all over the world have visited the site to pay homage and remember. The visit is often emotional, cathartic and ultimately affirming.

These visits and the clear *need* to know more led to the establishment of The Sixth Floor Museum. In working to preserve the site and establish the museum, the community leaders of Dallas sought to create an environment that recaptures the optimistic days of the Kennedy presidency, that is factual and forthright regarding the details of the assassination and that reveals the legacy of a president's life and tragic death.

This book is a powerful introduction to this sacred ground and, for those who visit Dealey Plaza, a powerful remembrance of the memories and emotions that the site evokes.

Memory pervades life. We devote much of the present to getting or keeping in touch with some aspect of the past. Few waking hours are devoid of recall or recollection; only intense concentration on some immediate pursuit can prevent the past from coming unbidden to mind.
•
DAVID LOWENTHAL

Aerial view of Dealey Plaza showing arrangement of streets, landscape features and surrounding buildings as they appeared on November 23, 1963. *Squire Haskins, courtesy Squire Haskins Photography, Inc.*

The sixth floor of the former Texas School Book Depository as it appeared before installation of The Sixth Floor Museum exhibit on the life, death and legacy of John F. Kennedy. *Sixth Floor Museum Archives*

President John Fitzgerald Kennedy (1917-1963) was assassinated by gunfire on November 22, 1963, while riding in a motorcade in Dallas, Texas. The shooting took place at 12:30 pm (CST) on Elm Street in Dealey Plaza, a vehicular park at the western edge of the central business district. His was the fourth presidential assassination in American history, the first in the nuclear age. The violent death of the leader of the strongest free nation in the world sent shock waves around the globe.

Today, more than three decades after the shooting, hundreds of millions still remember hearing the awful news of the death of the young American president. Some of them come to Dealey Plaza in search of resolution to lingering pain; younger visitors, unaffected by first-hand memory, visit the site seeking knowledge about a powerful and confusing event that changed the course of history.

Dealey Plaza, like Ford's Theater, Pearl Harbor and the Alamo, is a tragic historic site. It serves as a reminder that history is not necessarily celebration, that things sometimes go terribly wrong in America. George Santayana observed in 1905 that "those who cannot remember the past are condemned to repeat it." Dallas has preserved the Kennedy assassination site so that future generations can learn a powerful lesson from history.

The Sixth Floor Museum, located at 411 Elm Street in the former Texas School Book Depository, now the Dallas County Administration Building, provides educational insights into the life, death and legacy of John F. Kennedy. It is recommended that you begin your tour of the assassination site at the museum, which is open daily except December 25. An admission fee helps to offset the costs of operating the exhibits and research center, and assures preservation of the archival collections. Adult audio tours are available for rental in English, Spanish, French, Italian, Portuguese, German, and Japanese. The museum also offers rental audio tours in English for children under the age of twelve.

This guidebook provides an overview of the museum exhibits, followed by a walking tour of the assassination site, which contains a minimum of interpretive signage. You will also find information about nearby historic and cultural attractions, and a brief listing of books for further reading.

History, after all, is the memory of a nation.

•

JOHN F. KENNEDY
1917-1963

The Sixth Floor Museum

Visitors began coming to Dealey Plaza on the afternoon of November 22, 1963, to pay tribute to the memory of a slain president. The trend continued through the decades, fostered by Kennedy's strong legacy of hope, and the enduring controversy surrounding the reasons for his death. (*Figure 1*) After the assassination, Dallas engaged in a massive building program that completely changed the downtown skyline, but few changes were made to Dealey Plaza. Today, the park appears much as it did in 1963.

In 1970 the Texas School Book Depository Company moved out of the warehouse, where officials had found a rifle and spent bullet cartridges after the assassination. The structure was sold to a promoter from Nashville, Tennessee, who announced plans to develop a commercial JFK museum there. Shortly before the new owner defaulted on his note payments in 1972, an arsonist set fire to the building without success. The Dallas city council then denied a request for a permit to raze the old warehouse. Finally, in 1977, Dallas county residents approved the use of bond funds to purchase the building; the sixth floor was set aside, and Dallas County converted five other floors into a new seat of administrative government. The adaptive reuse was completed in phases between 1979 and 1988. In 1981 the building was renamed the Dallas County Administration Building.

A private, for-profit museum operated from 1970 until 1981 at the Dal-Tex Building across Houston Street from the old Depository. Even before this commercial museum closed, community leaders took tentative steps to provide some educational information for the public on the sixth floor of the former Depository, which overlooks the assassination site itself. Dallas County, working with community volunteer Lindalyn Bennett Adams, developed a plan to convert the sixth floor of the building into a history museum devoted to an examination of the life, death and legacy of John F. Kennedy. In 1983, the non-profit Dallas County Historical Foundation was incorporated to organize the museum and to operate it for the benefit of the public.

Most of the funds for the $3.8 million project were provided by organizations and individuals in Dallas County. Plans for the museum proved controversial with the public, since some feared that the display would commemorate the actions of Lee Harvey Oswald, Kennedy's alleged assassin. Nevertheless, in 1989 The Sixth Floor Museum

Seeing history on the ground is a lot less self-conscious process than reading about it.
•
HISTORIAN DAVID LOWENTHAL
The Past is a Foreign Country,
1985

History

FIGURE 1
Visitors from around the globe began coming to Dealey Plaza shortly after the assassination in 1963. Today, more than two million visitors come to the park each year to commemorate the memory of John F. Kennedy. *Ronald D. Rice, Sixth Floor Museum Archives*

opened to the public to positive reviews. More than 420,000 visitors, drawn from all parts of the United States and eighty foreign countries, tour the award-winning displays annually. The experience has proved cathartic for those who remember 1963, and educationally enriching for those born in the years following the tragedy. One local visitor wrote in the museum's memory books; [Thank you for giving us] "a dignity in remembering."

In addition to its permanent exhibit program, the museum is in the process of establishing a full research center, a state-of-the art archival storage facility, and a program of temporary exhibits. Museum staff responds to hundreds of requests for information each year from around the globe. The museum also plays an active role in assuring the on going preservation of the assassination site for the educational enrichment of future generations.

The Museum Tour

This [museum] has taken a very painful tragedy and given us [as] a city, people and a nation a dignity in remembering.

•

JEAN HILL, DALLAS
*Inscription in the Memory Book
February 17, 1989*

The Sixth Floor Museum is accessible from a visitor center located on the north side of the former Depository. The center can be reached from Houston Street near Pacific Avenue. Normal hours are 9:00 am until 6:00 pm daily, except December 25; check exterior signs for extended hours during the summer. The price for adults is $4.00; seniors (65+), $3.00; youths (6-18), $2.00. Children under six are admitted free. Audio tours rent for $2.00; the tour lasts thirty-seven minutes. Capacity on the sixth floor is restricted to 300 visitors, so visitors may experience a short wait. The average self-guided tour takes ninety minutes.

The museum contains 350 historic photographs and several dozen artifacts, including the original sniper's window and the scale model of the assassination site prepared in 1964 for the Warren Commission by the FBI. The displays include six documentary films, four of them in kiosks and two in small seated theaters. The two areas on the sixth floor where evidence was found have been restored and contain replicas of the boxes that were present on the day of the assassination. They are enclosed in glass to protect the historic flooring. (*Figure 2*)

No original evidence is included in the exhibits; all of it is housed at the National Archives in Washington, D.C. Graphically violent visuals associated with the assassination are not on display out of concern for the sensitivity of children. Due to copyright restrictions, no photography is allowed on the sixth floor. The visitor center has a security detector at the entrance; no weapons are allowed in the museum.

Although I wasn't born when this horrible act occurred, I have been touched by the incident. Mr. and Mrs. Kennedy will always be a part of my life....I am very moved by this wonderful exhibit. Thank you for preserving it so that I have a better understanding of that day.

•

JACQUELINE S. SPRING
Inscription in the Memory Book, October 31, 1994

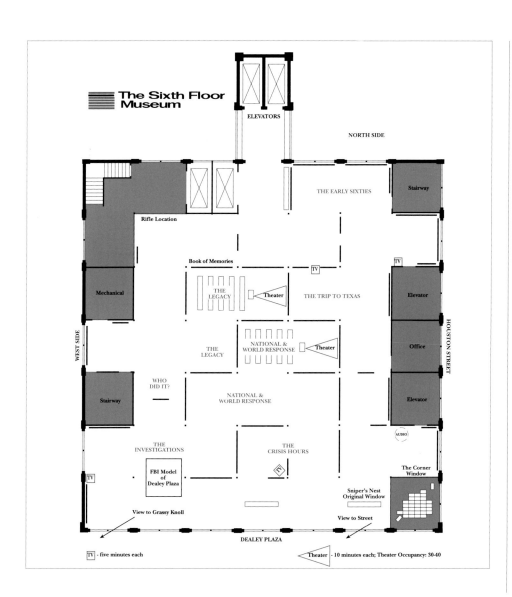

FIGURE 2
Floor plan of The Sixth Floor
Museum. *Staples & Charles Ltd.,
Sixth Floor Museum Archives*

The Early 60's

John F. Kennedy announced his bid for president on January 2, the second day of the new decade. For the next three years his programs and his style dominated the American scene. The period from 1960 to 1963 was a time of national transition between the stable traditionalism of the Eisenhower era and the radical unrest that followed Kennedy's death.

At his inaugural on January 20, 1961, Kennedy issued a challenge to "a new generation of Americans" to help him "get this country moving again." For the first time in American history, nearly half the population was under the age of twenty-five; Kennedy's youth and idealism appealed to this young audience. They liked his liberal New Frontier program and its promise of dramatic change. (*Figure 3*)

FIGURE 3
Section of the museum exhibits dealing with the early 1960's.
Sixth Floor Museum Archives

The American people expect more from us....For the world is changing. The old era is ending. The old ways will not do.

•

JOHN F. KENNEDY
July 15, 1960

A NEW GENERATION

John F. Kennedy's inaugural address was a clarion call for public commitment. (*Figure 4*) His New Frontier program was a set of challenges for Americans of all ages and persuasions to get involved with their country and to rediscover a national purpose. Many of the nation's youth took Kennedy at his word, entered public service and showed an interest in their country and the global human condition.

American youth during the Kennedy Administration was hardly rebellious. Despite earlier hints of unrest in the writings of Jack Kerouac and Allen Ginsberg, satirical preaching by comedian Mort Sahl, and images of wildness symbolized by actor Marlon Brando's leather jackets, most young people were preoccupied with Elvis Presley, rock and roll music, and the Twist, the dance craze of the era.

"Camelot" opened on Broadway, movie-goers reveled in images of Marilyn Monroe and Elizabeth Taylor, and art critics debated the merits of Pop Art. "The Dick Van Dyke Show" and "The Twilight Zone" were popular television shows. Major motion pictures included "Psycho," "Lawrence of Arabia," "Tom Jones," and "Where the Boys Are." Soft pop music kept pace with rock and roll during the early years of the decade. Surfing and protest music slowly gained in popularity.

Color television, air conditioning and clothes dryers were innovations for most American consumers. McDonald's had appeared on the American scene, but fast food was not yet a staple in the national diet. During the early 1960's, secretaries converted to the new automatic IBM Selectric typewriter and camera buffs tried Polaroid color film.

Most laymen pondered the implications of new discoveries and inventions: lasers, quasars, ICBM's, tetracycline, birth control pills, DNA and the first mechanical heart. In 1962, the Supreme Court banned compulsory prayer in public schools. As a result of the Vatican II Council the same year, English

Let the word go forth . . . that the torch has been passed to a new generation of Americans.

•

JOHN F. KENNEDY
*Inaugural Address
January 20, 1961*

FIGURE 4
Chief Justice Earl Warren, right, shown administering the oath of office to John F. Kennedy, January 20, 1961. *Courtesy John F. Kennedy Library*

replaced Latin as the language used in U.S. Catholic churches. In 1963 there were about 4,200 computers in use in the United States.

THE 1960 CAMPAIGN

John F. Kennedy served fourteen years in the Congress before he ran for president in 1960. Senators Hubert H. Humphrey of Minnesota and Lyndon Baines Johnson of Texas were his main Democratic opponents during the hard-fought primaries. After Kennedy won the party's nomination in July, he faced incumbent Vice President Richard M. Nixon in the general election in November. Lyndon Johnson was selected as Kennedy's running mate, a move to gain southern support for the Massachusetts senator's campaign.

Kennedy's age—he was forty-three—and his Catholicism became major issues early in the campaign. Some detractors decried his lack of maturity, while others warned that the U.S. had never had a Catholic chief of state; Rome would rule the nation, they warned. The Democratic senator's liberal New Frontier platform, drawing on Franklin D. Roosevelt's New Deal and Harry S. Truman's Fair Deal, called for sweeping new social and economic programs. Kennedy was charismatic with voters, a quality apparent to millions when he and Richard M. Nixon participated in the first televised presidential debates in September and October. Robert F. Kennedy managed his older brother's campaign.

On election night JFK retired for the evening without knowing the final voting results. When the returns were tallied, he had won by less than 120,000 nationwide votes out of a total of 69,000,000 cast. On January 20, 1961, John F. Kennedy was sworn in as the thirty-fifth president of the United States. Inauguration day was chilly but festive. Top hats, tails and a poetry reading by Robert Frost set the tone for the new administration's style. Kennedy's inaugural address was particularly stirring. "Ask not what your country can do for you," he said, "ask what you can do for your country."

THE KENNEDYS

The second of nine children born to Joseph P. and Rose Fitzgerald Kennedy, John F. Kennedy grew up in a wealthy and powerful Irish Catholic family in Boston,

We stand today on the edge of a new frontier—the frontier of the 60's, a frontier of unknown opportunities and paths, a frontier of unfulfilled hopes and threats . . . . I believe the times demand invention, innovation, imagination, decision.

•

SENATOR JOHN F. KENNEDY
*Nomination Acceptance Speech
July, 1960*

• *Rose Fitzgerald Kennedy, matriarch of the family, died in 1995 at the age of 104. She outlived her husband and four of her children: Joe Jr., Kathleen, John, and Robert.*

FIGURE 5

The Kennedy family in England. From left:
Rose, Ted, Rosemary, Joe Jr., Ambassador
Joseph Kennedy, Eunice, Jean, John,
Robert, Patricia, and Kathleen. *Courtesy*
Gilbert Adams/Camera Press/Retna Ltd.

Massachusetts. By the time Kennedy was born in 1917, the Kennedys had been active in Boston politics for decades. John F. "Honey Fitz" Fitzgerald, his maternal grandfather, served in the Congress and as mayor of Boston. Joseph P. Kennedy served as ambassador to the court of St. James in London from 1938 to 1940. (*Figure 5*) Ambassador Kennedy groomed his eldest son Joseph for a career in politics, but Joe was killed in 1944 during service in World War II. Educated at Choate and Harvard, John F. Kennedy served in the Navy during the war and was decorated for heroism after his PT-109 boat was sunk in the Solomon Islands. JFK then won a seat in the House of Representatives as a Democrat from Massachusetts in 1946, and was elected to the Senate in 1952.

Senator Kennedy was among America's most eligible bachelors when he married Newport, Rhode Island, socialite Jacqueline Lee Bouvier (1929-1994) in September, 1953. Jackie, as she was popularly known, was raised among the aristocracy of New York and Newport, graduated from Miss Porter's private school in Hartford, and attended Vassar and George Washington University. The couple met at a dinner party in Georgetown. Their Newport wedding in 1953 was the society event of the season. (*Figure 6*)

The Kennedys had one stillborn child before daughter Caroline was born in 1957. John Jr. was born in 1960 shortly after his father's election to the presidency. Young Patrick Bouvier was born in 1963, but the infant died of respiratory complications after only a few days. The family often relaxed at the Kennedy compound at Hyannis Port, Massachusetts, where touch football and sailing were favorite sports.

> *For of those to whom much is*
> *given, much is required.*
> •
> JOHN F. KENNEDY
> *January 9, 1961*

FIGURE 6

Jacqueline Bouvier and John F.
Kennedy with attendants at their
society wedding in Newport, R.I.,
in 1953. *Courtesy UPI/Bettmann*

*The pay is good and
I can walk to work.*

•

JOHN F. KENNEDY

FIGURE 7
"Probably a two o'clock feeding."
*Jerry Marcus, courtesy John F. Kennedy
Library*

FIGURE 8
A White House dinner honoring
America's Nobel laureates in 1962.
Jacqueline Kennedy is shown
speaking with poet Robert Frost.
*Robert Knudsen, courtesy John F.
Kennedy Library*

THE KENNEDY WHITE HOUSE

The new president and his family introduced a youthful spirit into the White House, and the nation followed their activities avidly. (*Figure 7*) The New Frontier administration became identified with style. High fashion, French food, cocktails and superb entertainment were signatures of the Kennedy era.

The Kennedys and the arts became synonymous during the early 1960's. They continued earlier efforts to create a national cultural center, and youth performances at the White House promoted artistic endeavors for America's young people. (*Figure 8*) Leading artists performed at official dinners, and Jacqueline Kennedy placed the redecoration of the Executive Mansion in the national spotlight. Her televised "White House Tour" in 1962 was watched by millions. Kennedy created the nucleus of both the National Endowment for the Arts and for the Humanities, programs that were formally established during the administration of his successor, Lyndon Johnson.

John F. Kennedy's popularity with the media proved helpful in keeping him in the public eye. He averaged one press conference every seventeen days in office. Americans enjoyed Kennedy's wit, and although many did not endorse his New

Frontier program, there was a general fascination with his style, his good looks and his energetic approach toward the office of the presidency.

JFK tapped a broad range of talent to assist him in inaugurating a new era of change. His cabinet was bipartisan and generally young, including Ford Motor Company chief Robert McNamara as secretary of defense, and Rockefeller Foundation president Dean Rusk as secretary of state. The most controversial appointment was Kennedy's selection of his brother Robert as attorney general. In response to accusations of nepotism, JFK quipped that the job would give Bobby some experience before the youthful attorney went out to practice law. Kennedy also turned to noted academicians, businessmen, economists, and political theorists who served as informal advisors to prepare reports on policies and programs. Campaign staffers Theodore Sorensen, Lawrence O'Brien, Kenneth O'Donnell and Dave Powers were among the trusted associates invited to serve in the new administration. Political wags called them the "Irish Mafia."

ECONOMIC AND SOCIAL PROGRAMS

During Kennedy's presidency the nation's economy flourished. Economist Walter Heller, chairman of the Council on Economic Advisors, favored induced federal deficits at a time of economic growth to overcome high unemployment, a radical departure from the balanced-budget philosophy of the previous administration. The same economic approach later became the backbone of Reaganomics during the 1980's. The deficit was roughly $286 billion in January, 1963.

The administration moved against a threat of recession in 1961 by introducing the first major minimum-wage law since 1938. The 1962 Trade Expansion Act was designed to boost exports and aid the economy. JFK's sweeping 1963 tax reduction program was passed by his successor, Lyndon B. Johnson. American business generally viewed Kennedy's economic policies as anti-business and harshly criticized the president for pressuring the steel industry into repealing a price increase in 1962.

Massive new social programs were central to Kennedy's New Frontier philosophy. He introduced legislation to combat mental retardation and to improve health, education and housing. Approval for many of these programs stalled in the conservative

Anti-White House sentiment in business circles had not been so virulent since financiers raged against FDR in the 1930's.

•

COLUMNIST JAMES RESTON
The New York Times

Congress. The Wilderness Act, passed in 1964, protected vast American natural resources and promoted interest in conservation of the environment.

Kennedy's international programs, the Peace Corps and the Alliance for Progress, called for sending American knowledge and technology to underdeveloped nations. The Peace Corps Act of 1961 employed Americans as volunteers in foreign lands. It continues today. (*Figure 9*) The 1961 "Alianza para el Progreso," a massive ten-year economic and social aid program for Latin America, was less successful and did not live up to expectations.

TURMOIL AT HOME

The drive for racial equality matured during the early 1960's. Violence broke out in the southeast in 1961 during restaurant sit-ins and Alabama freedom rides. Civil rights leaders urged the president to introduce legislation to end discrimination against African-Americans. Kennedy hesitated.

FIGURE 9
Peace Corps volunteer Delores Tadlock served in India. *Courtesy Peace Corps*

> *Americans are free to disagree with the law, but not to disobey it . . . no man . . . no mob . . . is entitled to defy a court of law.*
>
> •
>
> JOHN F. KENNEDY
> *September 30, 1962*

> *Two—four—one—three, we hate Ken-ne-dy.*
>
> •
>
> WHITE CHANT OUTSIDE
> UNIVERSITY OF MISSISSIPPI
> *September 30, 1962*

JFK lacked support for the issue in the Congress, so for two years he took positive action through the executive branch of government by enforcing court-ordered desegregation, pushing for the elimination of discriminatory poll taxes, appointing African-Americans to more government jobs, and creating the Committee on Equal Employment Opportunity.

In 1962 and 1963 the administration sent in federal troops to force integration at the University of Mississippi and the University of Alabama. On June 19, 1963, Kennedy submitted an omnibus civil rights bill, the largest since Reconstruction, to the Congress. On August 28, 1963, a crowd of 200,000, led by civil rights leader Dr. Martin Luther King Jr. marched peacefully on Washington, D.C., where Dr. King made his famous "I have a dream" speech. (*Figure 10*) After the rally, President Kennedy met with King and the other organizers. Many southern conservatives opposed the civil rights bill. As a result the president's popularity fell in national polls.

Right and left-wing extremist groups were another source of domestic turmoil. Ultra-conservative groups believed that Kennedy was soft on communism. They also

FIGURE 10

On August 28, 1963, the Rev. Dr. Martin Luther King Jr. led more than 200,000 civil-rights activists in a peaceful demonstration in Washington, D.C. Here, the crowd at the Lincoln Memorial, where Dr. King delivered his famous "I have a dream" speech. *Courtesy AP/Wide World Photos*

FIGURE 11

Officials used attack dogs and fire hoses against civil rights demonstrators in 1963 in Birmingham, Alabama. *Courtesy UPI/Bettmann*

condemned his civil rights program. (*Figure 11*) The radical left, including pro-Castro factions, believed that the administration was war mongering. Robert Kennedy angered labor leaders and organized crime with an aggressive Justice Department program against the mob and its influence on American labor unions.

We will bury you!

•

SOVIET PREMIER NIKITA
KHRUSHCHEV
*Speech at the United Nations
1960*

Figure 12
Soviet Premier Nikita Khrushchev,
shown pounding his fist on the
table during an appearance at the
United Nations in New York, 1960.
Courtesy AP/Wide World Photos

THE RED THREAT

Kennedy's presidency was dominated by the cold war, a delicate balance of power between the world's two nuclear giants, the communist Soviet Union and the democratic United States. The launching of Sputnik I in October 1957 placed the Soviets ahead in space technology, a potential military risk, and the administration feared communist threats in Cuba, Berlin, Southeast Asia and other parts of the world.

The Kennedy administration promoted the largest peacetime defense build-up in history, prior to the administration of Ronald Reagan, and promised to halt the global spread of communism. In 1961 Kennedy approved a CIA-backed invasion of Cuba. Cuban refugees entered the island at the Bay of Pigs to incite local riots and overthrow President Fidel Castro. The invasion failed miserably. John F. Kennedy accepted full responsibility for the foreign policy fiasco.

In 1961 Soviet Premier Nikita Khrushchev threatened to sign a peace treaty with Soviet-controlled East Germany, a move that would have blocked access to West Berlin, which remained a free city according to the terms worked out after World War II. (*Figure 12*) During August the communists erected the Berlin wall to prevent citizens of the eastern part of the city from escaping to the west. American and Soviet troops squared off at the wall, but no open hostilities ensued. The treaty was postponed.

For thirteen days in October 1962, the world stood on the brink of possible nuclear war after American intelligence services discovered that the Soviet Union was building offensive missile sites on Cuba. The administration issued a blockade against ships carrying missile parts to the island; tensions escalated until the Soviets agreed to dismantle the bases if the United States pledged not to invade Cuba. Kennedy's popularity at home soared.

We and the communists are locked in a deadly embrace all around the world.

•

JOHN F. KENNEDY
October, 1960

The Kennedy administration continued direct American involvement in Vietnam. It sent financial aid to South Vietnam, and Kennedy created the Special Forces (Green Berets), who taught guerrilla warfare and other tactics to Vietnamese troops. He increased the number of American advisors there from 5,000 to nearly 17,000. Shortly before his death in 1963, JFK announced that he would reduce the number of American forces by 1,000.

After the Cuban missile crisis, Soviet-American relations began to thaw. A Nuclear Test Ban Treaty with the Soviets was signed in 1963. Kennedy considered the treaty his greatest achievement. The famous "hot line" to Moscow was established the same year. Despite these early moves toward detente, the fear of communist world domination was profound in America during the entire period that JFK was in office.

THE SPACE RACE

Troubled by Soviet domination in space after the launch of Sputnik I in 1957, John F. Kennedy took steps after his inauguration to speed up American exploratory efforts. He named Vice President Lyndon B. Johnson as chairman of the National Space Council and asked Congress to channel billions of dollars into a new space program designed to place an American on the moon within a decade.

This major commitment to space exploration boosted American technology and led to the first Project Mercury manned space flight by Alan Shepard in 1961, followed by the first orbital flight by John Glenn in 1962. These successes were followed by the launch of an unmanned space probe past Venus.

Kennedy signed the Satellite Communications Act in 1962, and in July the first Telstar satellite relayed television programs between the United States and Europe. Telstar increased American dominance in international communications. The new satellite and space technology was applied to other fields, including medicine, metal fabrication and weapons research.

. . . this nation should commit itself to achieving the goal, before this decade is out, of landing a man on the moon and returning him safely to the earth.

•

JOHN F. KENNEDY
May 25, 1961

The Trip to Texas

It was presidential politics pure and simple. It was the opening effort of the 1964 campaign. And it was going beautifully.

•

LYNDON B. JOHNSON
The Vantage Point, *1971*

In November 1963, President Kennedy began a political trip to five Texas cities. He and native son Lyndon B. Johnson had carried the state by a narrow margin in 1960, and the president wanted to shore up support and raise funds for his reelection bid in 1964. A split between liberals and conservatives within the state's dominant Democratic party was making matters worse. Kennedy hoped to smooth a rift between liberal Texas Senator Ralph Yarborough and conservatives who backed Democratic Governor John B. Connally.

In a departure from her preferred pattern, Jacqueline Kennedy accompanied the president. It was her first public tour since the death of the couple's infant son Patrick on August 9, 1963. Lady Bird Johnson accompanied the vice president. Governor John Connally and his wife Nellie Connally served as hosts to the presidential party.

The itinerary included visits to San Antonio, Houston, Fort Worth, Dallas, and Austin, with motorcades planned for each stop. Although each city made extensive preparations for the presidential visit, John F. Kennedy's tendency to mingle with

FIGURE 13
Early on the morning of November 22, 1963, President Kennedy made an appearance outside the Hotel Texas in Fort Worth to deliver remarks to a crowd that had gathered there.
*William Allen/*Dallas Times Herald *Collection, Sixth Floor Museum Archives*

crowds created difficult security risks. But Texans greeted him enthusiastically everywhere.

Air Force One flew to San Antonio on November 21, where Kennedy dedicated a new aerospace medical center. The president then proceeded to Houston and delivered a speech at Rice University. That evening the Kennedys attended a dinner honoring Houston Congressman Albert Thomas and were guests at a meeting of the League of United Latin American Countries (LULAC), where Jacqueline Kennedy delighted the audience with impromptu remarks in Spanish.

The presidential party left Houston late on November 21, arriving at Fort Worth's Hotel Texas at 11:30 pm. Early the next morning, Kennedy crossed the street in the rain and addressed an enthusiastic crowd. (*Figure 13*) Later Mrs. Kennedy joined him at a breakfast for 2,500 citizens sponsored by the Fort Worth Chamber of Commerce. At 11:20 am *Air Force One* left Fort Worth's Carswell Air Force Base on the short flight to Dallas. The weather had cleared and Kennedy remarked to Connally, "it looks as if we'll get sunshine." JFK had ordered the non-bullet-proof top on his limousine removed.

RECEPTION IN DALLAS

Plans for the Dallas segment of the trip called for an open motorcade from Love Field through downtown Dallas, before the presidential party attended a sold-out luncheon for 2,600 citizens at the Dallas Trade Mart, located just west and north of the downtown area.

In 1963 Dallas had a metropolitan population of one million people, and was the business and financial center of the state. "Big D" had developed a reputation for conservatism, having voted Republican in the 1960 election. Small ultra-conservative extremist groups, including the John Birch Society and the Indignant White Citizens Council, were active in the community.

In November 1960, LBJ and his wife had been heckled by a crowd outside the Adolphus Hotel in downtown Dallas. On October 24, 1963, United Nations Ambassador Adlai Stevenson was spat upon and hit with a placard while he was in Dallas to deliver a United Nations Day speech. The Stevenson attack made national news. (*Figure 14*)

FIGURE 14

United Nations Ambassador Adlai Stevenson was hit on the head by a placard on October 24, 1963, during a Dallas appearance. Stevenson blamed what he called a small "idiot fringe" in the city for the incident and later wrote to a Kennedy advisor that he believed Dallas would give "an enthusiastic and sincere" reception to the president.
Courtesy AP/Wide World Photos

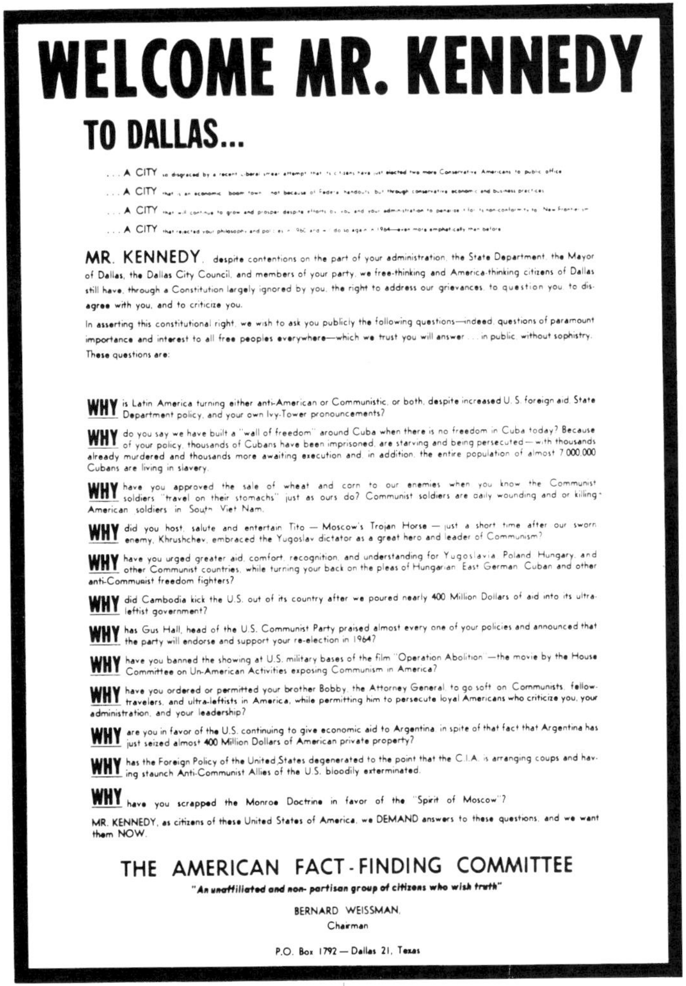

WELCOME MR. KENNEDY

TO DALLAS...

...A CITY so disgraced by a recent liberal smear attempt that its citizens have just elected two more Conservative Americans to public office

...A CITY that is an economic boom town - not because of federal handouts, but through conservative economic and business practices

...A CITY that will continue to grow and prosper despite efforts by you and your administration to penalize it for its non-conformity to New Frontierism

...A CITY that rejected your philosophy and policies in 1960 and will do so again in 1964 - even more emphatically than before

MR. KENNEDY, despite contentions on the part of your administration, the State Department, the Mayor of Dallas, the Dallas City Council, and members of your party, we free-thinking and America-thinking citizens of Dallas still have, through a Constitution largely ignored by you, the right to address our grievances, to question you to disagree with you, and to criticize you.

In asserting this constitutional right, we wish to ask you publicly the following questions—indeed, questions of paramount importance and interest to all free peoples everywhere—which we trust you will answer ... in public, without sophistry. These questions are:

WHY is Latin America turning either anti-American or Communistic, or both, despite increased U.S. foreign aid, State Department policy, and your own Ivy-Tower pronouncements?

WHY do you say we have built a "wall of freedom" around Cuba when there is no freedom in Cuba today? Because of your policy, thousands of Cubans have been imprisoned, are starving and being persecuted—with thousands already murdered and thousands more awaiting execution and, in addition, the entire population of almost 7,000,000 Cubans are living in slavery.

WHY have you approved the sale of wheat and corn to our enemies when you know the Communist soldiers "travel on their stomachs" just as ours do? Communist soldiers are daily wounding and/or killing American soldiers in South Viet Nam.

WHY did you host, salute and entertain Tito - Moscow's Trojan Horse - just a short time after our sworn enemy, Khrushchev, embraced the Yugoslav dictator as a great hero and leader of Communism?

WHY have you urged greater aid, comfort, recognition and understanding for Yugoslavia, Poland, Hungary, and other Communist countries, while turning your back on the pleas of Hungarian, East German, Cuban and other anti-Communist freedom fighters?

WHY did Cambodia kick the U.S. out of its country after we poured nearly 400 Million Dollars of aid into its ultra-leftist government?

WHY has Gus Hall, head of the U.S. Communist Party praised almost every one of your policies and announced that the party will endorse and support your re-election in 1964?

WHY have you banned the showing at U.S. military bases of the film "Operation Abolition"—the movie by the House Committee on Un-American Activities exposing Communism in America?

WHY have you ordered or permitted your brother Bobby, the Attorney General to go soft on Communists, fellow-travelers, and ultra-leftists in America, while permitting him to persecute loyal Americans who criticize you, your administration, and your leadership?

WHY are you in favor of the U.S. continuing to give economic aid to Argentina in spite of the fact that Argentina has just seized almost 400 Million Dollars of American private property?

WHY has the Foreign Policy of the United States degenerated to the point that the C.I.A. is arranging coups and having staunch Anti-Communist Allies of the U.S. bloodily exterminated?

WHY have you scrapped the Monroe Doctrine in favor of the "Spirit of Moscow"?

MR. KENNEDY, as citizens of these United States of America, we DEMAND answers to these questions, and we want them NOW.

THE AMERICAN FACT-FINDING COMMITTEE

"An unaffiliated and non-partisan group of citizens who wish truth"

BERNARD WEISSMAN
Chairman

P.O. Box 1792 — Dallas 21, Texas

Dallas officials were concerned about possible protests against Kennedy's civil rights bill, which had cost him a great deal of support in the conservative south. Community leaders called for a dignified reception for the president. Security for the visit was the tightest in the history of the city, with more than 200 police officers stationed at the cavernous Trade Mart luncheon site. Planners were alarmed on the morning of November 22 when *The Dallas Morning News* carried a full-page advertisement protesting the president's policies. (*Figure 15*) Nevertheless, the visit began well.

Air Force One touched down at Love Field in Dallas at 11:37 am. A crowd of nearly four thousand people met the Kennedys at the airport and, after brief ceremonies with local officials, the president and first lady moved along the fence to shake hands with the enthusiastic crowd. Then they joined the Connallys in the president's open limousine for the parade through downtown Dallas. (*Figure 16*) The motorcade left Love Field at 11:50 am, traveling downtown via Mockingbird Lane, Lemmon Avenue, Turtle Creek Boulevard, Cedar Springs Road and Harwood Street. At Harwood the vehicle turned west onto Main Street, the heart of the city's business district.

FIGURE 15

Anti-Kennedy advertisement which appeared in *The Dallas Morning News* on November 22, 1963, the day that JFK was scheduled to visit the city. *Sixth Floor Museum Archives*

FIGURE 17
The Kennedy motorcade shown moving through the downtown Dallas crowds, estimated at 200,000. Dallasites gave an enthusiastic welcome to the president. *William Beal/*Dallas Times Herald *Collection, Sixth Floor Museum Archives*

FIGURE 16
The Kennedys and Connallys in the presidential limousine as the motorcade prepared to leave Love Field Airport. *Tom C. Dillard, Sixth Floor Museum Archives*

More than 200,000 people had gathered downtown to offer a hearty welcome to the presidential party. (*Figure 17*) President and Mrs. Kennedy occupied the rear seats of the big Lincoln Continental limousine with Governor and Mrs. Connally in the jump seats in front of them. The ladies sat on the side behind the driver. Vice President and Mrs. Johnson rode behind the president in another open convertible. The temperature was in the mid-60's. Sunshine had replaced the early morning drizzle.

*...there was no danger
whatsoever and none in evidence
of adverse reactions to
the president's visit....a completely
overwhelming welcome
for the president!*

•

Bob Huffaker,
*KRLD Radio Reporter
November 22, 1963
as the limousine approached
Dealey Plaza*

*Mr. President, you can't say
Dallas doesn't love you.*

•

Nellie Connally
*November 22, 1963 12:29 pm
Just after the limousine turned onto
Houston Street in Dealey Plaza*

Figure 18
The limousine, shown here,
turning from Main onto Houston
Street at the entrance to Dealey
Plaza. The time was 12:29 pm.
The arrow points to LBJ's location.
*Phil Willis, Copyright 1964.
Updated to 2039*

THE ASSASSINATION

At the western end of Main Street the parade passed into Dealey Plaza, a rectangular park with three streets—Main in the center, Commerce on the south and Elm on the north—that converged beneath a railroad bridge known as the triple underpass. At Houston Street the presidential limousine turned north for one block and then wheeled left onto Elm Street toward the triple underpass. (*Figures 18, 19*) The turn was necessary in order to gain access to the ramp leading onto Stemmons Freeway, the main highway connecting downtown to the Trade Mart, site of the luncheon honoring the president.

Although the parade was officially over, there were several hundred people in Dealey Plaza. More than two dozen of them had cameras to record the Kennedys' visit to the city. Dress manufacturer Abraham Zapruder was among them with an 8mm Bell & Howell movie camera. He stood on a plinth at the colonnade north of Elm Street.

As the limousine slowly made the left turn from Houston onto Elm Street, it passed directly beneath the Texas School Book Depository. The large clock on the Hertz advertising sign atop the building recorded the time as 12:30 pm. Shortly after the Lincoln Continental completed the turn, a shot rang out. (*Figure 20*) At first, many witnesses believed the sound was a backfire. Dallas motorcycle policeman Bobby Hargis, who was riding to the left rear of the presidential limousine, thought; "God, let it be a fire-cracker." The car was moving in the middle lane at about eleven miles per hour.

Then, another shot. Suddenly, bystanders realized that some-one was shooting at the president. JFK's arms rose; he was clearly wounded. Mrs. Kennedy turned to look at him in alarm. Governor Connally suddenly

FIGURE 19
As the limousine made the turn from Houston Street onto Elm, it slowed down. The Dal-Tex Building is shown here in the background. *James M. Towner, courtesy Tina Towner Wanner*

FIGURE 20
Frame 161 of the 8mm film taken by Dallasite Abraham Zapruder. The limousine had made the turn onto Elm Street and was moving toward the triple underpass when the first shot rang out. *Abraham Zapruder, copyright LMH Company, 1967*

FIGURE 21
A view of the presidential limousine a fraction of a second after President Kennedy's head exploded. The grassy knoll appears in the background. *Mary Moorman, courtesy Mary Ann Moorman Krahmer and AP/Wide World Photos*

appeared wounded and shouted, "Oh no, no, no," before Nellie Connally pulled him down into her lap. The president's car slowed to a crawl; meanwhile, Secret Service Agent Clint Hill left the running board of the follow-up security car and sprinted toward the president.

Another shot rang out, exploding a portion of the president's head. (*Figure 21*) Nearby witnesses fell to the ground, desperate to get out of the line of fire. Mrs. Kennedy climbed out on the trunk of the limousine and grasped a piece of her husband's head. She was joined there by Agent Hill, who leapt onto the trunk just as the car accelerated and sped from Dealey Plaza. (*Figure 22*) The first lady crouched

FIGURE 22
After the fatal shot, Mrs. Kennedy climbed onto the trunk of the limousine; Secret Service Agent Clint Hill, shown here, finally reached the car. *Orville Nix film copyright 1963, 1990; courtesy Gayle Nix Jackson*

FIGURE 23

The limousine shown racing at top
speed to Parkland Hospital after
the shooting. *Al Volkland/*Dallas
Times Herald *Collection, Sixth Floor
Museum Archives*

down, cradling her husband's body, while the limousine raced at speeds of 70–80 mph
to Parkland Hospital, the region's leading trauma center. Agent Hill rode spread eagle
on the trunk, pounding his fists in frustration. "There was no screaming in that
horrible car," recalled Nellie Connally. "It was just a silent, terrible drive." (*Figure 23*)

The shooting was over in six to eight seconds. City police and county sheriff's
deputies streamed into the park to look for suspects and evidence, and to interview
the stunned witnesses.

THE INITIAL SEARCH

Dallas motorcycle policeman Marrion L. Baker was riding in the motorcade on Houston Street behind the presidential party, heard shots, and saw pigeons flying off the roof of the Depository. Gunning his engine, he headed toward the building. Inside the entrance Baker met building superintendent Roy Truly, and together they began to search for a gunman. The upper floors were accessed by two freight elevators and a staircase, all on the north side of the warehouse. The elevators were stopped on upper floors, so Baker and Truly ran up the stairs in the northwest corner.

On the second floor Baker spotted a man inside an employee lunchroom and stopped him at gunpoint for questioning. The time was about 12:32 pm. Baker released the suspect when Truly identified Lee Harvey Oswald as an order clerk for the company; he had been hired five weeks earlier. Oswald apparently walked out the front door of the building around 12:33 pm.

Officers converged on the Depository and began a floor-by-floor search of the dimly-lit warehouse. Shortly after 1:00 pm Truly took a "roll call" of employees. Oswald turned up among the missing workers, and police initiated a search for him. At 1:12 pm investigators discovered a barricade of boxes and a rifleman's perch in the southeast corner on the sixth floor facing Dealey Plaza. The perch contained three spent bullet cartridges, finger and palm prints later identified as Oswald's, and a paper bag that officials said was used to carry a rifle into the building. (*Figures 24, 25*)

At 1:22 pm Dallas County Deputy Sheriff Eugene Boone discovered a rifle with a telescopic sight and a cartridge clip hidden between boxes near the staircase in the

Crisis Hours

Three shots were fired at President Kennedy's motorcade today in downtown Dallas.

•

MERRIMAN SMITH
UPI Reporter
Report from motorcade
November 22, 1963
12:34 pm (CST)

I then went...direct to the far corner and then discovered a cubbyhole...constructed out of cartons which protected it from sight and found where someone had been in an area of perhaps 2 feet surrounded by cardboard cartons of books.

•

DEPUTY SHERIFF LUKE MOONEY
Affidavit taken November 22, 1963

FIGURE 25
Dallas homicide investigators,
shown leaving the Depository on
November 22 with the paper
bag said to have been used to
transport the murder rifle into
the building. *William Allen/*Dallas
Times Herald *Collection, Sixth Floor
Museum Archives*

FIGURE 24
The sniper's perch, discovered at 1:12 pm (CST) on the sixth floor of the Texas School
Book Depository. *Sixth Floor Museum Archives*

FIGURE 26
Dallas Police Lt. Carl Day points to the location of the rifle on the sixth floor of the
Depository. It was hidden between book cartons near the corner staircase on the northwest
side of the building. *William Allen/*Dallas Times Herald *Collection, Sixth Floor Museum Archives*

northwest corner of the sixth floor. (*Figure 26*) Dallas police later found a partial palm print of Oswald's beneath the rifle stock; federal officials traced ownership of the 1940 Italian Mannlicher-Carcano to Oswald. Government investigators later argued that a sniper could have fired the shots, run to the corner staircase and descended to the second floor lunchroom in less than two minutes.

At the same time that Officer Baker was entering the Depository, several other witnesses led investigators to another possible sniper location, the rail yards north of the grassy knoll. Police found only cigarette butts and footprints in the area behind the stockade fence there. The search of this area was discontinued when evidence was found in the Depository.

THE SNIPER'S PERCH

One of the two main areas on the sixth floor where evidence was found, this corner has been restored to its 1963 appearance, and is set off by glass to protect the historic flooring. The boxes are reproductions of the ones found by investigators shortly after the assassination. (*Figure 27*) Their arrangement is a close approximation,

FIGURE 27
A view of the reconstructed sniper's perch in The Sixth Floor Museum.
Sixth Floor Museum Archives

FIGURE 28
Display case housing the original
window from the sniper's perch
on the sixth floor of the old
Depository; the artifact was
removed for safekeeping in 1963
by building owner Col. D. Harold
Byrd and returned on loan to The
Sixth Floor Museum by his son,
Caruth C. Byrd, in 1994. *Bret St.
Clair, Sixth Floor Museum Archives*

*The news spread like some
deadly contagion.*

•

MOLLIE PANTER-DOWNES
from London
The New Yorker, *December 7, 1963*

based on a film and photographs taken on the day of the shooting. Officials disturbed the layout during their investigation.

The window, displayed in a case nearby, was removed from the far corner window six weeks after the assassination by building owner Colonel D. Harold Byrd, who was concerned about the possibility of vandalism. Col. Byrd kept the window in his home, and it was inherited by his son, Caruth C. Byrd, who returned it to The Sixth Floor Museum in 1994. "I thought long and hard about what to do with this window," said Caruth Byrd at ceremonies that accompanied the unveiling of the historic artifact, "I finally decided that the only thing to do would be to bring it back home." Note the original pinkish exterior paint color on the sash; the exterior trim was changed back to its 1901 dark green color when the building was restored between 1979 and 1981. (*Figure 28*)

FIRST REPORTS

The wire services spread news of the shooting worldwide within a matter of minutes. Most Americans knew that the president had been shot before they heard the dreadful confirmation of his death at 1:33 pm. (*Figure 29*) During the weekend that followed, the average American watched over thirty-two hours of television. For the

FIGURE 29
Assistant White House Press Secretary
Malcolm Kilduff, right, shown making
the official announcement of President
Kennedy's death at 1:33 pm. Dallas
Times Herald *Collection, Sixth Floor
Museum Archives*

first time, networks canceled all advertising and devoted continuous coverage to the news.

The limousine arrived at Parkland Hospital at 12:36 pm. President Kennedy and Governor Connally were rushed into separate rooms for treatment by experienced trauma teams. Connally survived surgery for bullet wounds to his back, chest, wrist and thigh. A rib and his wrist had been broken in the shooting. Doctors were unable to save President Kennedy, who had a bullet wound in his neck below the Adam's apple and a massive head wound. After a priest administered the Last Rites, JFK was pronounced dead at 1:00 pm. Lyndon B. Johnson automatically became the new president.

A SUSPECT APPREHENDED

Alerted to the shooting of Dallas patrolman J.D. Tippit in the Oak Cliff section of the city at about 1:15 pm, police searched the area and arrested Lee Harvey Oswald in the Texas Theater at 1:50 pm. He was armed with a pistol and tried to shoot a Dallas policeman during the arrest. (*Figures 30, 31*) Oswald, 24, was charged with the death of

FIGURE 30
The scene on Tenth Street where Dallas Police officer J.D. Tippit was shot and killed at about 1:15 pm on November 22, 1963. An officer stands where Tippit fell near his squad car, as investigators and witnesses gather. *Darryl Heikes/* Dallas Times Herald *Collection, Sixth Floor Museum Archives*

FIGURE 31
Lee Harvey Oswald, center, shown outside the Texas Theater shortly after his arrest for the murder of policeman J.D. Tippit on November 22, 1963. *James MacCammon, courtesy Howard Upchurch, Sixth Floor Museum Archives*

I'm just a patsy.

•

LEE HARVEY OSWALD
November 22, 1963

This case is cinched.

•

DALLAS HOMICIDE DETECTIVE
WILL FRITZ
November 23, 1963

FIGURE 32
During his interrogation by investi-
gators, Oswald steadfastly denied
any involvement in the deaths
of Officer Tippit or President
Kennedy. He is shown here at
Dallas police headquarters on
November 22, 1963. *Bill Winfrey/
Tom C. Dillard Collection, Sixth
Floor Museum Archives*

Officer Tippit. Later, Dallas police also charged him with the murder of the president.

During the weekend, investigators amassed a wealth of circumstantial evidence against Oswald. He was an ex-Marine who had defected to the Soviet Union and re-entered the United States with a Russian wife. During military service, Oswald had qualified as a sharpshooter (a medium proficiency level), but his grade slipped to the lower level of marksman during his final test. Officials determined that Oswald owned the rifle and the pistol used to shoot officer Tippit; police found his finger and palm prints in the sniper's perch and on the assassination weapon. Two witnesses said Oswald had carried a paper bag, presumably containing his rifle, with him to work on the morning of the assassination. Oswald stated repeatedly that he was innocent of both murders. (*Figure 32*)

Reporters jammed police headquarters during the weekend, shouting questions at police and the suspect. Some leaders voiced concerns that the heavy national publicity might undermine the suspect's chances for a fair trial. At 11:21 am on Sunday, November 24, Oswald was shot by Dallas nightclub owner Jack Ruby, while police prepared to transfer the suspect from the city to county jail. The shooting, which took place in the basement of Dallas Police headquarters, was carried live on NBC television. (*Figure 33*) Oswald died during surgery at Parkland Hospital at 1:07 pm.

Jack Ruby was immediately taken into custody and stood trial in Dallas in March 1964, for the murder of Lee Harvey Oswald. Once again, media from around the world descended on Dallas. The Dallas nightclub owner maintained that he had shot Oswald to spare Jacqueline Kennedy and her small children the ordeal of a trial. The jury convicted Ruby of murder, but the ruling was later overturned on appeal, based on issues of venue and admission of evidence. Jack Ruby was diagnosed with cancer in 1966 and died early in 1967 before his new trial.

The interrogation [of Oswald] was a three ring circus.

•

DALLAS POLICE CHIEF JESSE CURRY
JFK Assassination File, *1969*

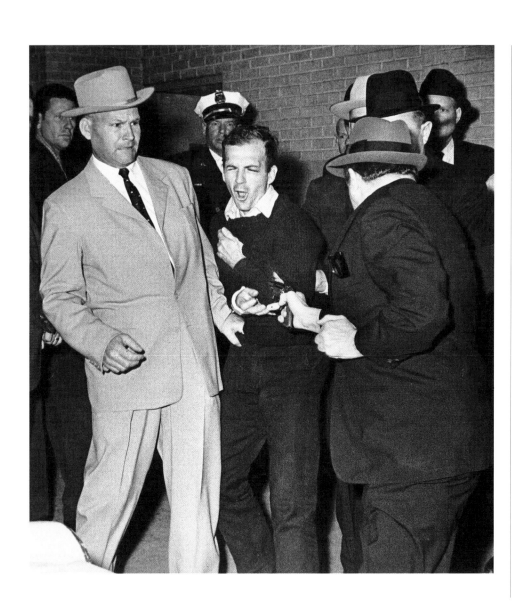

FIGURE 33

Dallas nightclub owner Jack Ruby
shot assassination suspect Lee
Harvey Oswald at 11:21 am on
November 24, 1963. The shooting
took place in the basement of
Dallas Police headquarters.
Oswald was being transferred from
the city to the county jail, pending
trial. The suspect died during
surgery at Parkland Hospital
at 1:07 pm. *Copyright 1963
Bob Jackson*

I do solemnly swear that I will faithfully execute the office of President of the United States, and will to the best of my ability, preserve, protect, and defend the Constitution of the United States. So help me God.

•

LYNDON BAINES JOHNSON
2:38 PM
Aboard Air Force One
November 22, 1963

FIGURE 34
President Lyndon Johnson being escorted from Parkland Hospital after the shooting. Johnson returned to *Air Force One*, which had better security and advanced communications systems. Dallas Times Herald *Collection, Sixth Floor Museum Archives*

THE OATH OF OFFICE

Aides told the vice president of John F. Kennedy's death at 1:00 pm. Fearing a wide-spread conspiracy, government agents urged Johnson to return immediately to Washington. Half the presidential cabinet was airborne en route to a conference in Tokyo, and the military had placed the country on red alert. Although the plane carrying the cabinet members turned around immediately, there was no leader officially in charge in the nation's capital. (*Figure 34*)

Johnson refused to leave Dallas without Mrs. Kennedy, who refused to leave without her husband's body. Assassinating the president of the United States was not a federal crime in 1963, so the responsibility for the autopsy and investigation fell under local and state authority. Texas law required an autopsy in all violent deaths, before a body could be released to next of kin. Kennedy staffers refused to let the slain president's body remain for an autopsy in Dallas, so it was forcefully removed and put aboard *Air Force One*, where President Johnson had been taken for security reasons.

At 2:38 pm Federal District Judge Sarah T. Hughes, a Kennedy appointee, administered the oath of office to President Johnson. Reaffirming the commitment to "preserve, protect, and defend the Constitution" was not required by law, but every vice president since John Tyler had followed the custom. Security agents had sealed the windows and exits aboard *Air Force One*, so the swearing-in took place in the sweltering presidential cabin aboard the plane. Mrs. Kennedy attended the ceremony, still wearing the blood-spattered pink suit that she had worn in the motorcade. Aides

FIGURE 35
Federal Judge Sarah T. Hughes, a Kennedy appointee, administered the oath of office to Lyndon Johnson aboard *Air Force One* at 2:38 pm. Mrs. Kennedy attended the brief ceremony, then retired to the rear of the plane to sit with her husband's coffin. *Cecil W. Stoughton, courtesy Lyndon Baines Johnson Library*

urged her to change her clothes, but she refused. "Let them see what they have done," she said. (*Figure 35*)

As soon as he had taken the oath, Johnson issued the order for take-off and *Air Force One* returned to Andrews Air Force Base near Washington, D.C. There LBJ gave a brief address, concluding with the words, "I ask for your help, and God's." President Kennedy's remains, accompanied again by Jacqueline Kennedy, were taken to Bethesda Naval Hospital for an autopsy.

THE NATION AND WORLD RESPOND

The initial global reaction to news of the assassination was shock, then grief. Cars stopped on streets, businesses and schools closed. Entertainments were canceled everywhere. It was the first American presidential assassination since 1901. "Americans don't assassinate their presidents," exclaimed one shocked British television commentator.

At home, people gathered around radios or television sets. Churches opened their doors for prayer. Foreign embassies and consulates were flooded with people offering condolences. (*Figure 36*) One Japanese family walked eighteen miles to the American embassy in Tokyo to pay its respects. Flags in foreign nations dropped to half staff. Even before official notices could be sent, scores of world leaders wired the State Department that they would attend the funeral ceremonies in the capital on Monday, November 25, declared by President Johnson as a national day of mourning.

The assassination caused more than two thirds of the American people to experience some physical symptoms of illness and emotional distress. At home and abroad most compared the loss of the American leader to that of a family member or close friend.

> *The sense of stunned grief and dismay at John Kennedy's death has made the greatest break thus far in the iron curtain.*
>
> •
>
> COLUMNIST MAX LERNER
> New Statesman, *December 23, 1963*

> *What a terrible thing has happened to us all!. . . We mourn with you poor, sad American people.*
>
> •
>
> IRISH POET SEAN O'CASEY
> *Letter to a friend*
> *November 25, 1963*

FIGURE 36
A group of young Argentineans shown delivering a bouquet in memory of JFK to the American embassy in Buenos Aires.
Courtesy National Archives

FIGURE 37
Dallasites were stunned by the
assassination and placed hundreds
of floral tributes in Dealey Plaza.
Bill Winfrey, courtesy The Dallas
Morning News

*She gave an example to the
whole world of how to behave.*

•

FRENCH PRESIDENT
CHARLES DEGAULLE
*November 25, 1963
Describing Jacqueline Kennedy*

Dallas was chastised for mishandling the investigation, and some blamed the city for the assassination itself. "We are a tormented town," said one Dallas civic leader. The helpless local citizenry placed hundreds of memorial tributes to John F. Kennedy in Dealey Plaza. (*Figure 37*) On Sunday the football game between the Dallas Cowboys and the Cleveland Browns took place as scheduled. Announcers in the Ohio stadium did not introduce either team for fear that the crowd would boo the Dallas players.

FUNERAL IN WASHINGTON

Television made it possible for the entire nation, and millions in foreign lands, to attend the funeral of John F. Kennedy in Washington, D.C. on November 25, 1963. People found solace in the dignified ceremony, which included 7,000 members of the military and was attended by more than 100 leaders from foreign countries. Many other nations scheduled memorial services to coincide with the official rites in Washington.

Scenes of the young widow with her daughter kneeling at the president's bier, of the riderless horse Black Jack, the flag-draped coffin, and Mrs. Kennedy leading world leaders on foot behind the funeral procession made a lasting impression on the global viewing audience. (*Figure 38*) Jacqueline Kennedy's remarkable self-control helped unify the nation and added poignancy to the services. Her leadership during the weekend became the most important part of her legacy.

Mrs. Kennedy arranged for the ceremony to be modeled after the Lincoln state funeral held a century earlier. John F. Kennedy's casket lay in state in the East Room at the White House on Saturday. After private services the family received official visitors. On Sunday the slain president's casket was taken to the rotunda at the Capitol for a

She was a patriot, who all by herself one terrible weekend lifted and braced the heart of a nation.

•

PEGGY NOONAN
Time, *May 30, 1994*

congressional memorial service. There, Kennedy's bier remained for public viewing; hundreds of thousands of people filed by to pay their respects.

On Monday morning, the casket was returned to the entrance of the White House. There the Kennedy family and dignitaries joined behind the caisson and marched on foot to St. Matthew's Cathedral for a mass. Jacqueline Kennedy led the march. After the funeral and another procession, John F. Kennedy was buried at Arlington National Cemetery on a hillside overlooking the Lincoln Memorial. At the conclusion of the service, his widow lit an eternal flame to mark the place. (*Figure 39*)

During the ceremonies in Washington, people paused worldwide to pay their respects to the fallen American president. Salutes were fired at thousands of American military bases around the world. Ships tossed memorial wreaths into the sea; the Panama Canal closed; Greek police stopped all traffic, and Manhattan cab drivers abandoned their vehicles to bow their heads. For the only time in its history the Associated Press teletype machines fell silent.

After the funeral, the Kennedys received guests in the White House. That night, Jacqueline Kennedy hosted a small birthday party for John F. Kennedy Jr. It was his third birthday. (*Figure 40*)

FIGURE 39
A 1964 view of the grave site of John F. Kennedy at Arlington National Cemetery. *Courtesy John F. Kennedy Library*

FIGURE 38
Jacqueline Bouvier Kennedy, accompanied by Robert Kennedy (left) and Ted Kennedy (right) led the march on foot to her husband's funeral at St. Matthew's Cathedral in Washington, D.C., on November 25, 1963. *Robert Knudsen, courtesy John F. Kennedy Library*

FIGURE 40
John F. Kennedy Jr., age three, shown saluting his father's caisson after the funeral on November 25, 1963. *Courtesy UPI/Bettmann*

The Investigations

On November 29, 1963, President Johnson created the President's Commission on the Assassination of President Kennedy, chaired by Supreme Court Chief Justice Earl Warren. The panel came to be known as the Warren Commission. The commission's *Report* and twenty-six volumes of testimony and exhibits were released in September and November, 1964. (*Figure 41*) The conclusion: Lee Harvey Oswald, acting alone, killed the president. Accepted at first, the *Report's* inconsistencies later launched a controversy that has led to more than three decades of inquiry and spirited public debate.

FIGURE 41

On November 29, 1963, President Johnson appointed a panel to investigate the Kennedy slaying. From left: John J. McCloy, Chief Counsel J. Lee Rankin, Sen. Richard B. Russell, Rep. Gerald R. Ford, Chief Justice Earl Warren, former CIA Director Allen W. Dulles, Sen. John Sherman Cooper, and Rep. Hale Boggs present the report to President Johnson on September 24, 1964.
Courtesy Lyndon Baines Johnson Library.

The investigation of the assassination...will undoubtedly be the most thorough job of research in modern history. If a nation cannot believe the findings of this investigation, then there is little it can believe.

•

EDITORIAL
Dallas Times Herald
December 4, 1963

Between 1966 and 1978 four government panels undertook additional examinations of the medical evidence. Collectively, they concluded that the president was hit by two shots fired from behind and revealed that the Warren Commission *Report* had erred significantly in the placement of both wounds.

During the mid-1970's, the presidential Rockefeller Commission and the senate's Church Committee probes into United States intelligence activities disclosed that the FBI, CIA and Secret Service had all withheld information from the Warren Commission, including the fact that during the early 1960's the CIA and Mafia had cooperated in plans to assassinate Fidel Castro. These findings further eroded confidence in the original Warren Commission findings. Public demand grew for an independent congressional investigation into John F. Kennedy's death.

Between 1964 and 1976 hundreds of books and articles criticizing the Warren Commission *Report* were published; conspiracy theories flourished. In 1975 Americans, disgruntled by government due to the Watergate scandal, were shown an enhancement on television of the 8mm film of the assassination photographed by Abraham Zapruder; a violent backward movement of the president's head and body suggested that the fatal shot had been fired from the front. In 1976 Congress created the House Select Committee on Assassinations to investigate the Kennedy and Martin Luther King Jr. slayings.

The House Committee supported the Warren Commission's earlier finding that Oswald killed the president, but concluded in 1978 that he was part of a larger plot. The committee ruled that acoustical analyses determined, with a probability of 95% or better, that two gunmen fired at the motorcade, one from the Depository and an unknown sniper from the grassy knoll. Based on medical evidence from the autopsy performed at Bethesda, the committee determined that the shot from the grassy knoll had missed the occupants of the limousine. A government-sponsored report issued in 1982 disagreed with the House panel's acoustic interpretation. In 1988 the Justice Department announced that there was "no persuasive evidence" of conspiracy and closed the Kennedy and King investigations.

In 1991, Hollywood film maker Oliver Stone released "JFK," a pro-conspiracy movie based on the remembrances of New Orleans District Attorney Jim Garrison, who

The year 2000 will see men still arguing . . . about the president's death.

•

JOURNALIST HARRISON SALISBURY
The New York Times
1964

F IGURE 42
Official photograph showing
the three spent bullet cartridges
found on the floor of the sniper's
perch in the Texas School Book
Depository. *Sixth Floor Museum
Archives*

launched a criminal conspiracy investigation into the assassination during the late
1960's. Garrison's case fell apart, but Stone's controversial film aroused interest among
young Americans in calling for release of all classified documents pertaining to JFK's
assassination. In 1992 legislation was approved for appointment of a presidential review
board to oversee the declassification process.

The conclusions reached by major official investigations are summarized below:

Early Investigations, 1963-1964: Texas local and state investigators
turned over witness testimony and physical evidence to the FBI,
after President Johnson created the Warren Commission on
November 29, 1963. (*Figure 42*) The FBI also conducted its own
investigation and submitted a four-volume report on December 9
with a supplement on January 13, 1964. A Secret Service inquiry
included over 1,400 interviews and a reenactment of the assassination. Its report was delivered to the FBI on December 18,
1963. The FBI and Secret Service concurred that Oswald was the
lone killer.

The FBI became the main investigative agency for the
Warren Commission. The Bureau's early report concluded that
three shots were fired at the presidential limousine; the first and
third hit the president and the second wounded Governor
Connally. Connally agreed. As Connally told CBS television in
1967: "The first bullet did not hit me. The second bullet did hit
me. The third bullet did not hit me." The FBI found no exit for
the president's back wound, a point of controversy later.

The Warren Commission, 1963-1964: After Oswald's murder,
52% of the country believed that the assassination was the result
of a conspiracy. The Warren Commission used existing investigative agencies, hired a staff of lawyers and submitted its *Report* to
the president in ten months. The commission concluded that

Oswald fired three shots at the limousine from the sixth floor corner window of the Depository. One shot missed, said the commission, and there was "persuasive evidence" that one shot hit President Kennedy in the back of the neck and passed through him to cause several injuries to Governor Connally. The third shot hit the president in the head and killed him.

Ownership of the rifle and partial finger and palm prints found at the scene tied Oswald to the crime, and the commission ruled that he had a capacity for violence, based on the evidence linking him to the death of patrolman Tippit. The commission found no evidence of conspiracy. It recommended reorganization of the Secret Service, legislation making it a federal crime to assassinate the president or vice president, and voluntary procedures for the media and law enforcement agencies to protect a suspect's right to due process.

The Clark Panels, 1966 and 1968: The president's autopsy was performed at Bethesda Naval Hospital on November 22-23, 1963. The Warren Commission did not examine the autopsy X-rays or photographs, an omission that contributed to doubt about the validity of its conclusion that bullets entered the president's neck and head from the rear.

Attorney General Ramsey Clark convened two panels to review the original medical evidence. The panels upheld the commission findings on the number and direction of shots, but located the entry wound to the head four inches higher. (*Figures 43, 44*) No visuals were submitted with their reports.

The Rockefeller Commission, 1975: The President's Commission on CIA Activities Within the United States, chaired by Vice President Nelson Rockefeller, disclosed illegal domestic activities performed by the agency and included eighteen pages

FIGURES 43, 44
Compare the different government conclusions about the nature of President Kennedy's head wound. Figure 43, left, shows a drawing made for the Warren Commission, indicating that a bullet entered low on the rear of Kennedy's head. Figure 44, right, reflects the findings of the Clark and later medical panels, which concluded that the bullet entered four inches higher on JFK's head. *Based on Warren Commission CE 388 and HSCA JFK F-65, National Archives*

FIGURE 45

A 1976 Senate probe about U. S. Intelligence agencies revealed that the FBI, Secret Service and the CIA had all withheld information from the Warren Commission, which might have led the presidential panel to further investigate the issue of possible conspiracy. *Tony Auth in the* Philadelphia Inquirer.

discussing allegations of possible CIA involvement with the assassination of John F. Kennedy. It found no credible evidence of CIA complicity in the crime. The Rockefeller Commission's medical panel also supported the Warren Commission's original findings that the president was killed by bullets fired from the rear.

The Church Committee, 1976: The Senate Select Committee to Study Governmental Operations with Respect to Intelligence Activities, chaired by Senator Frank Church, looked further into the CIA/assassination issue. The Church Committee's *Report* found no evidence of CIA complicity in the Kennedy assassination. However, the committee determined that the CIA enlisted the Mafia in a plot to assassinate Fidel Castro during the early 1960's and withheld this information from the Warren Commission. It also determined that the FBI, CIA and Secret Service had withheld information from the Warren panel "which might have substantially affected the course of the investigation." (*Figure 45*) Demand grew for a new official investigation.

The House Select Committee on Assassinations, 1976-1978: The House Select Committee on Assassinations, an inquiry into the Kennedy and King slayings, issued its *Report* with twenty-seven volumes of testimony and exhibits in 1979. The committee relied heavily on scientific analyses of original evidence, including acoustical analysis of a police recording which might have included sounds of the Kennedy assassination.

The committee's *Report* supported the Warren Commission's finding that Oswald fired three shots. The House Committee's conclusions: the first shot missed; the second hit the president and wounded Governor Connally; the third shot hit the president in the head and killed him. Acoustical analysis established, with a probability of 95% or better, that a second gunman fired from behind the fence on the grassy knoll; this shot missed. Kennedy was probably killed as a result of a conspiracy by unidentified individuals. The committee's *Report* criticized the work of the Warren panel and some of the investigative agencies it used.

Acoustical Report, 1982: In 1980, the Justice Department asked the National Academy of Science to convene a panel to review the acoustical analysis developed for the House Select Committee. The National Research Council's *Report* of the Committee on Ballistics Acoustics, issued in 1982, offered the following conclusions: the House acoustic analysis did not demonstrate that there was a shot fired from the grassy knoll; there was no basis for concluding a 95% probability of such a shot; crosstalk on the recording indicated that the sound patterns appeared about one minute after the assassination, while other sounds suggested that the open microphone was located near the Trade Mart. G. Robert Blakey, former director of the House Select Committee, went on record requesting further studies as a means to clarify the difference of opinion among the scientific community. (*Figure 46*)

THE FBI MODEL OF DEALEY PLAZA

The scale model prepared for the Warren Commission by the FBI was based on information gathered in Dealey Plaza on December 2, 3, and 4, 1963. The completed exhibit was installed at the offices of the Warren Commission on January 20, 1964. The model played an important role in the Warren Commission investigation and was also used less extensively during the House Select Committee probe between 1976 and 1978. Early in 1995, the National Archives in Washington, D.C., agreed to loan the artifact to The Sixth Floor Museum. (*Figure 47*)

FIGURE 46
Scientific analysis of acoustic sounds recorded in Dallas on November 22, 1963 led the House Select Committee to perform a reenactment of the shooting at Dealey Plaza in 1978. Shots were fired into sand bags from the sixth floor window of the Depository and from behind the picket fence on the grassy knoll. Microphones were stationed at intervals to record the sounds. Comparisons led the House Committee to conclude that two gunmen fired on the motorcade. *Courtesy The Dallas Morning News*

FIGURE 47
A view of the FBI model as installed in The Sixth Floor Museum. The agency prepared the model of the assassination site and presented it to the Warren Commission early in 1964. The House Select Committee also used the model during its investigation in 1976-1978. The model is on loan from the National Archives. *Bret St. Clair, Sixth Floor Museum Archives*

The model was designed to be a working exhibit with movable cars and pedestrian figures. Strings were attached to Elm Street at the presumed location of the presidential limousine at the time that shots were fired, then drawn back to the sixth floor corner window in order to determine trajectories.

Contemporary photographs of the model in use indicate that in January 1964 the FBI misunderstood how the assassination had taken place. For example, the visual record clearly showed that when the fatal head shot hit President Kennedy, the limousine was in front of the location of Abraham Zapruder. The Warren Commission adopted this conclusion and issued an opinion that it was doubtful that any shots were fired after the bullet struck the president in the head.

The 1964 photographs accompanying the model show that the FBI marked the fatal shot to the head at a location that coincided with the second shot fired from the Depository. This error is in conflict with the FBI's own official report, issued six weeks before completion of the model, that it was the third shot, and not the second, that struck JFK in the head. Perhaps the FBI division assigned to build the model was not in communication with another FBI division working on determining the sequence of shots.

The museum has placed the limousine, following cars and many bystanders in their correct positions for the fatal shot (*Figure 47*). Note the location of the coiled strings on the street; they remain in the location that the model builders used in 1964 to indicate the location of the presidential limosine for each of the shots. The FBI did not arrange the pedestrian figures to show their locations at the time of the shots, so the museum used film and photographs to place them in their approximate locations at the time the fatal shot hit the president.

THE EVIDENCE: FORENSIC & BALLISTIC

Texas investigators, the FBI and the Secret Service all felt that there was sufficient evidence to charge Oswald with the president's murder. The Warren Commission used their material, plus witness testimony, ballistic test firing of the rifle, trajectory analysis and forensic data to conclude that Oswald fired three shots from the sixth floor corner window of the Depository, and that two shots caused all the wounds to

To say that they [Kennedy and Connally] were hit by separate bullets is synonymous with saying that there were two assassins.

•

WARREN COMMISSION COUNSEL
WARREN REDLICH
1965

FIGURE 48

The nearly pristine bullet found on a stretcher at Parkland Hospital about 1:45 pm on the day of the assassination. Two government probes concluded that this bullet was fired from Oswald's rifle, and both agreed that it caused wounds to President Kennedy and Governor Connally. Although the missile is deformed, critics have long questioned how this bullet could break bones and retain so much of its original shape. Neutron Activation Analysis performed on the bullet in 1977 proved that the bullet fragments taken from Governor Connally's wrist came from this bullet, but the researchers questioned the authenticity of the fragments themselves. *Warren Commission CE 399, courtesy National Archives*

Kennedy and Connally. A "near-pristine' bullet, found on an abandoned stretcher at Parkland Hospital at around 1:45 pm on the day of the assassination, was determined to have been fired from Oswald's rifle; it was this bullet, said the commission, that had caused Kennedy's neck wound and all of the injuries to Governor Connally. (*Figure 48*) The commission also concluded that Oswald had murdered Officer J.D. Tippit.

Conflicting witness testimony about the origin and number of shots, confusion over the location of wounds, discrepancies in medical reporting, and skepticism that a "near-pristine bullet" could have caused wounds to both Kennedy and Connally led to immediate and continuing controversy about the validity of the commission's findings and the authenticity of the evidence itself. The Clark panels' finding that the Warren Commission had misplaced the location of the entry wound on the president's head by four inches only fueled the controversy. (*Figures 43, 44*)

Thirteen years of critical books, seminars and public demand for a re-opening of the investigation led to the House Select Committee's examination in 1976-1978. Using highly sophisticated scientific investigative procedures—some not available earlier to the Warren Commission—the House Committee upheld the Warren Commission's finding that Oswald shot the president and the governor from the sixth floor and concurred that one bullet wounded both men. The committee's medical

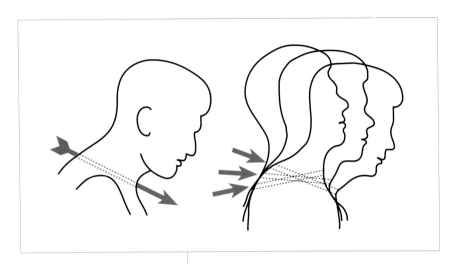

Figures 49, 50
The House Select Committee probe during the 1970's showed that the Warren Commission had also erred in the location of the president's back wound. On the bottom, the Warren Commission exhibit, indicating that the bullet entered at the base of JFK's neck and exited his throat. On the top, the House exhibits which show the bullet entering about five inches lower on JFK's back. All told, five medical panels convened between 1966 and 1978 agreed, by a majority, that all of the wounds to the president were fired from behind and above his location. *Based on Warren Commission CE 385 and HSCA JFK F-46, National Archives*

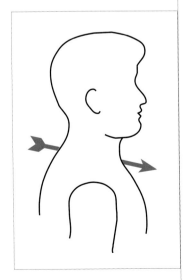

panel found that the entry point of the president's back wound was several inches lower than the Warren *Report* had indicated. (*Figures 49, 50*)

Forensics: The Back Wound. Parkland trauma teams used lifesaving methods and never turned over Kennedy's body to notice a back wound. They enlarged his frontal neck wound in a tracheotomy. Bethesda Naval Hospital doctors, led by Commander James Humes, performed the autopsy without consulting the Dallas doctors. Their probe of the back wound revealed no exit point; presumably the tracheotomy obscured it. Humes learned of the neck wound from one of the Dallas doctors the next day and changed his report accordingly.

No autopsy photographs or X-rays were used in preparing Humes' report, which conflicted with later commission exhibits showing the back wound entry point at the base of Kennedy's neck. The House Committee's forensic experts reviewed all medical evidence and concluded by a majority that a bullet came from the rear, entered Kennedy's upper right back, emerged from the neck and could have also caused Governor Connally's wounds.

Forensics: The Head Wound. An initial statement from JFK's personal physician stated that the president was hit in the temple, implying a shot from the front. News reports based on comments from the Parkland doctors supported this idea. The autopsy placed the entry wound on the lower back of the head, a conclusion accepted by the Warren panel. This apparent inconsistency fueled the controversy about the medical evidence.

The Clark panel determined that a bullet entered about four inches higher on the rear of the president's head, a location confirmed by the House Committee's medical panel. Scientific tests on two bullet fragments found in the limousine showed that they came from Oswald's rifle and had caused the head wound. The House Committee's trajectory analysis also confirmed the rear entry.

The Near-pristine Bullet: Ballistics tests showed that the 6.5mm bullet found on a stretcher at Parkland Hospital on November 22 came from the Oswald rifle. Based on probability analysis and trajectory tests, the Warren Commission developed, and ultimately accepted, the "single bullet theory," whereby this one bullet caused wounds to both President Kennedy and Governor Connally.

Critics promptly named the projectile the "magic bullet," and argued that it was planted. They also insisted that the condition of the missile was too good for it to have broken Connally's rib and shattered his wrist. The controversy led the House Committee to conduct reaction-time and alignment experiments, wound ballistic examinations and neutron activation analysis of the bullet. Its conclusions supported the Warren Commission single bullet theory.

Ballistics: Evidence found on the sixth floor included the rifle mounted with a telescopic sight, a cartridge clip and one live shell, three empty cartridge cases, a paper bag, and partial prints of Lee Harvey Oswald. Other ballistic evidence included the "near-pristine bullet," bullet fragments from the limousine and victims, a cracked windshield and dented frame from the limousine, and a marked curbstone from Main Street near the spot where witness James Tague was wounded on the cheek by an unidentified fragment.

Ballistic experiments demonstrated that the rifle could have produced the wounds. The Warren Commission confirmed Oswald's ownership of the rifle, the finger and palm print identifications and his probable presence in the corner window at the time of the shooting. The House Committee firearms panel concurred.

The Clock—The Zapruder Film: The 8mm film made by witness Abraham Zapruder, running at an average of 18.3 frames per second for a total of 22 seconds, was used by the Warren and House inquiries to help determine the timing of shots and the trajectories for wounds. The probes agreed on the issue of trajectories but differed on timing. The Warren Commission concluded that the shooting took place in about 5.6 seconds; the House Committee said it took 8.3 seconds. The FBI had refired the rifle, without aiming, for the Warren panel in 2.25 seconds. This statistic discouraged the commission from concluding that Kennedy had been hit in the back by the first shot and Connally by the second. The Zapruder film seemed to show both men reacting to wounds in less than 2.25 seconds. House experts fired another rifle in 1.67 seconds without using the telescopic sight, but embraced the single bullet theory for different reasons.

According to the Warren Commission, the first shot to hit was the near-pristine bullet, which struck both men. The commission said it was fired between Zapruder frames 210-224. The House concluded that Oswald's first shot (frame 161) had missed; his second shot was fired around frame 190, with Connally showing a reaction to this shot by frame 224. Connally maintained that he was hit by a separate bullet. Both panels concurred that Oswald fired the third and fatal shot at frame 312, and that the damage to President Kennedy's head appeared at frame 313. The House panel reported that a fourth shot, from the grassy knoll, was fired at frame 295 and missed.

THE EVIDENCE: PHOTOGRAPHIC & ACOUSTIC

The Warren Commission used some enhancement techniques to examine the photographic evidence, but scientific advances after 1964 enabled the House Select Committee to use new technology to evaluate visual evidence associated with the assassination.

As memories fade, technology progresses.

•

G. ROBERT BLAKEY
Director, House Select Committee on Assassinations
1979

The House Committee examined the 500 or more photographs originally investigated by the Warren Commission, plus the autopsy photographs and X-rays, and some additional photographs not made public in 1964. The House Committee also benefitted from independent scientific work done by researcher Robert Groden to clarify the Zapruder film. Committee scientists used new chemical and radioactive processes and digital enhancement techniques to remove blur and enhance contrast in some of the original images. They authenticated the photographs showing Oswald holding his weapons, which Oswald and many critics had insisted were fakes, and also examined images to see if there were visible human forms in the areas at the grassy knoll and sixth floor windows. (*Figure 51*)

Committee scientists examined a Dictabelt recording containing sounds transmitted from a policeman's motorcycle at the approximate time of the assassination. Technicians filtered sounds to remove engine noise and initially found six possible noise patterns that could have been gunshots. These patterns were matched with test shots fired and recorded in Dealey Plaza on August 20, 1978. Marksmen fired shots from both the sixth floor window and the grassy knoll. The comparison led to four correlations which, with further refinement using physics and geometry, led the House Committee to conclude that there was a shot fired from the grassy knoll.

According to committee scientists, the physical layout of Dealey Plaza created a measurable environment for sound waves, generating a "sound fingerprint" for the site and the assassination. Another government-sponsored evaluation of the House acoustical data, issued in 1982, disagreed with the committee scientists' conclusions. The Justice Department also discounted the House Committee's acoustical work when it closed the probe in 1988 without finding "persuasive evidence" of conspiracy.

FIGURE 51
The day after the shooting Dallas police discovered two photographs and two negatives among Oswald's possessions which showed him holding the weapons used in the Kennedy and Tippit murders. Oswald insisted that they were fakes. These, plus another photograph discovered after 1964 in a private collection, were analyzed for the House Select Committee, which ruled that all were genuine. *Warren Commission CE 133A, courtesy National Archives*

Who Did It?

I never believed that Oswald acted alone, although I can accept that he pulled the trigger.

•

LYNDON B. JOHNSON
Atlantic Monthly, July, 1973

Despite all the time and money spent on official and unofficial investigations since 1963, the Warren Commission's basic conclusion that Lee Harvey Oswald fired the shots that killed President Kennedy and wounded Governor Connally has never been disproved. Later government probes have supported this conclusion, and only one, Clay Shaw, of the fifty or more suspected snipers or conspirators offered by the critical community has been brought to trial; he was acquitted. Flaws in the Warren *Report* were caused, in part, by pressure for a quick solution to the crime in order to calm international anxiety. Also, the quality of the commission's work was weakened by the investigative agencies who withheld information from the Warren panel.

The questions "why?" and "for or with whom?" remain difficult. The Warren Commission made a strong case against Lee Oswald as a disgruntled left-wing loner capable of political murder, but the suspect's motives, if any, died with him, and no court of law ever convicted him. On the question of conspiracy, theories have ranged from the plausible to the ridiculous. Conspiracy theories have emerged after every presidential assassination in America, but the events of 1963 have spawned thousands of books and articles on the subject. Subsequent disclosures that investigative agencies withheld information from the Warren Commission have only fueled doubts among the public, which has increasingly questioned government credibility since the mid-1960's.

By the mid-1970's public opinion heavily favored the possibility of a plot without even identifying the conspirators. A 1973 Gallup Poll revealed that only 11% of the nation believed that Oswald had acted alone. A 1983 Gallup Poll yielded the same statistic. Despite lingering doubts about the assassination, 69% of the public surveyed in another poll in 1983 did not want to use tax dollars for another government investigation into the crime.

CONSPIRACY?

The Warren Commission ruled against the idea of a conspiracy. Although the House Select Committee investigation determined that Oswald was probably a part of a larger plot, it could not identify any individual conspirators. Since 1963 hundreds of conspiracy theories have been offered by critics of the government investigations. Many theorists felt that the Warren *Report* read more like a brief for the prosecution than an impartial analysis of Oswald's guilt or innocence. Some researchers have argued that Oswald was not at the scene of the crime, that evidence was planted to frame him, that he was a poor marksman, and that photographs showing him holding the murder weapons were faked. Speculation about an Oswald "double" led to the exhumation of his body in 1981. It was Oswald. National public opinion polls have shown that most Americans believe Oswald was the assassin or at least involved in the assassination. However, in the areas of possible conspiracy or unanswered questions, fully three quarters of the public do not ascribe to the official government position. (*Figure 52*)

Critics of government investigations have never adopted a uniform point of view on the issue of conspiracy, so the impact of the independent research community on public opinion has been cumulatively strong, but scattered as to the groups or individuals that are targets as potential plotters. The first generation of critics during the 1960's focused attention on discrepancies in the Warren *Report*. The second, prevalent during the late 1960's through the mid-1970's, developed elaborately complex scenarios for conspiracies involving the mob, the government, Cuban groups, etc. The decades since that time have seen volumes of material published about minutely-detailed aspects of certain conspiracies; today there are researchers who specialize in visual evidence, others who focus on medical evidence, and still others who concentrate on individuals who may or may not have been involved in a plot to kill the president. Some theories impugning government agents or agencies have been aimed at bureaucratic efforts to cover mistakes after the fact, rather than premeditated plots to kill the president.

The House Committee examined several major conspiracy theories and concluded that the most likely conspirators were individuals in the anti-Castro movement or individuals associated with organized crime. The committee criticized the Warren Commission and its investigative agencies for not looking more deeply into the issue of possible conspiracy, but found no American governmental involvement in a plot. In 1988 the Justice Department formally closed the House Committee investigation and cited "no persuasive evidence" of conspiracy.

FIGURE 52
The popularity of conspiracy theories in the JFK assassination has led many people to come forward since 1963 to claim that they were present on the grassy knoll at the time of the shooting. Noted assassination researcher Mary Ferrell was finally moved to comment that there were so many claims to a spot on the knoll that there was no longer any room for a sniper there. *Courtesy Jim Borgman. Reprinted with special permission of King Features Syndicate.*

Conspiracy theories have followed major trends in public debate. For example, during the height of the cold war it was the Soviet Union that topped the list of likely plotters. The disclosures during the mid-1970's about investigative agencies that withheld information from the Warren panel made the CIA or FBI favorite targets for blame, and Oliver Stone's 1991 blockbuster movie, "JFK," fostered a trend to blame JFK's murder on forces who did not want the U.S. to pull out of the costly war in Vietnam.

Psychologists have written that the American public has a tendency to seek a more important reason for the death of an American president than the deranged actions of a lonely little man. Oswald, they reason, may have been inadequate to the enormity of the crime; surely something bigger and more powerful was behind the death of JFK.

Some enduring theories are summarized below:

Soviet Government/KGB. Oswald's defection to Russia in 1959, and his residency there until 1962, raised immediate speculation that he became a KGB agent and killed the president for the Soviets. His marriage to the niece of a Soviet intelligence official only heightened such speculation. Neither the Warren Commission nor the House Select Committee found any evidence that Oswald was a KGB agent or that the Soviets had planned to kill the president. Since the fall of the Soviet Union in 1989, former KGB agents have come forward with information that discounts any communist plot against the thirty-fifth president.

The Cuban Government. Many people have suspected that Fidel Castro or the Cuban government was behind the assassination. Officials believed that Oswald tried to visit Cuba in 1963. Disclosures during the mid-1970's that the CIA had been involved in numerous plots to kill Castro—one using the Mafia—enhanced suspicion that the Cuban dictator might have ordered Kennedy's death in retaliation. The House Committee did not find any evidence of Cuban government retaliation against the U.S. plots or any high-level plans to kill Kennedy.

Anti-Castro Elements. Anti-Castro groups blamed John F. Kennedy for withdrawal of air support during the Bay of Pigs invasion in 1961, and his pledge not to invade Cuba after the 1962 missile crisis angered them further. There were more than 100 anti-Castro groups in the United States in November 1963; most of them were centered around Miami. The House Committee chastised the FBI and the Warren Commission for failing to pursue leads to anti-Castroites but cleared all groups, as groups, from any plot to assassinate the president.

FIGURE 53
New Orleans District Attorney Jim Garrison's (left) late-1960's probe focused on a conspiracy among Clay Shaw (second from left), David Ferrie (third from left), and Lee Harvey Oswald (right). Ferrie died before Garrison's case went to trial, but Shaw was tried and acquitted by a New Orleans jury in 1969. *Courtesy AP/Wide World Photos*

The House Committee did tie Oswald with several known anti-Castroites in New Orleans and Dallas. Oswald knew former FBI agent Guy Banister and pilot David Ferrie, an early target in New Orleans District Attorney Jim Garrison's 1967-69 conspiracy probe. One Dallas witness, Sylvia Odio, told investigators that a man she thought was Oswald was involved with an anti-Castro plot against Kennedy. The theme has remained popular with assassination researchers.

New Orleans Scenario. New Orleans District Attorney Jim Garrison announced in 1967 that he had uncovered a conspiracy involving a prominent local businessmen, Clay Shaw, to assassinate Kennedy. His original target was David Ferrie, a man known to Shaw, Oswald, and New Orleans Mafia chief Carlos Marcello. (*Figure 53*) Ferrie had been brought in for questioning in 1963 after Kennedy's assassination. Ferrie died before he was indicted, so Garrison turned to New Orleans businessman Clay Shaw as another prime suspect. Shaw was acquitted of any involvement in the assassination in 1969. Garrison's outspoken manner and questionable tactics earned him scorn, but his investigation gave support to conspiracy theorists and provided some important leads for the House Select Committee investigation that followed.

Jack Ruby. Ruby was tried and convicted for the murder of Lee Oswald in a Dallas trial in March 1964. The question of possible conspiracy was not an issue in his trial. Ruby won an appeal on admission of evidence and change of venue issues, but died of cancer in January 1967, before the new trial took place. Ruby told the Warren

Commission that he acted alone in the murder of Oswald in order to spare Mrs. Kennedy the ordeal of having to testify at a trial. (*Figure 54*) The commission concluded that Ruby did act alone and was not a member of organized crime.

The House Committee differed in its conclusion and found that the Chicago-born nightclub owner had ties with associates of New Orleans and Florida Mafia chieftains, and had made several trips to Cuba, apparently engaging in mob-related activities. The committee further concluded that Ruby had "stalked" Oswald prior to the November 24 shooting, which was executed, the committee suggested, like a Mafia "hit." The House Committee further reasoned that Ruby's financial difficulties might have led him to accept a mob contract to murder Oswald.

Organized Crime. The Warren Commission examined organized crime only as it related to Jack Ruby. Subsequent disclosures that the CIA had enlisted the mob in a plot to assassinate Fidel Castro led the House Committee to examine possible Mafia involvement more closely. The mob had strong motives against both John and Robert Kennedy, due to the Justice Department war against organized crime.

The House probe linked Oswald to associates of New Orleans Mafia chieftain Carlos Marcello; the *Report* cited David Ferrie and Guy Banister, both of whom were known to Oswald. Oswald's uncle and his mother also knew associates of Marcello.

The House Committee found that Ruby knew associates of both Marcello and Florida chief Santos Trafficante, a key figure behind the joint CIA/Mafia plot against Castro. The committee could not name any mob figures directly involved in a plot, nor could it link the assassination to any effort by a nationally organized criminal group. (*Figure 55*)

U.S. Investigative Agencies. Theorists have argued that a government agency planned the assassination. The Warren panel heard rumors that Oswald was a paid FBI informant, an allegation the Bureau denied. Later official inquiries revealed that the FBI and CIA withheld information from the Warren Commission. The House Committee determined that the FBI and CIA did not plan the assassination of President Kennedy and concluded that Oswald was not a government agent.

FIGURE 54
The media contributed to the
circus atmosphere around the
Dallas murder trial of Jack Ruby
in March 1964. Ruby (center)
is shown here surrounded by his
attorneys and reporters during
a rare interview. The night club
owner was given the death sentence and died of cancer in
1967 pending a new trial.
Tom C. Dillard, courtesy The Dallas
Morning News

The Warren Commission and the House Select Committee both criticized the Secret Service's performance before and during the assassination, but cleared the Service of any complicity in the crime. The House Committee concluded that Jack Ruby's familiarity with the Dallas Police Department may have led an officer to help Ruby gain access to the Oswald transfer, but all government probes cleared the Dallas Police of any involvement in a plot to kill the president.

Assassination researchers have also written extensively that rogue elements within American investigative agencies, particularly the CIA or FBI, were involved in planning the shooting. They are hopeful that declassification of previously-sealed government documents might shed light on this theme.

'THE COMMITTEE THANKS THE MAFIA FOR TESTIFYING IT DON'T NO WAY KNOW NOTHIN' ABOUT NO ASSASSINATIONS ... AND, THAT, I GUESS, WRAPS IT UP!'

FIGURE 55
The House Select Committee probe, and many private assassination researchers, have maintained that members of organized crime might have been involved in a plot to kill President Kennedy. The mob hated the Kennedy administration's anti-crime policy, and objected to the growth of detente in U.S./Cuban relations, since the Mafia once had profitable casino operations on the island. *Pat Oliphant, Sixth Floor Museum Archives*

The Far Right. Ultra-conservative groups such as the John Birch Society and the Minutemen were outspoken in their opposition to John F. Kennedy's policies. Several of these groups had spokesmen in Dallas, where the shooting took place. Theorists subsequently advanced the idea that the right-wing was behind a plot to kill the president. Neither the Warren Commission nor the House Select Committee found any evidence of a plot from these extremist groups or individuals.

Since Dallas was home to several vocal extremist elements in 1963, there were early public attacks against the community and some of its citizens. After the assassination the Warren Commission and House Committee dismissed these allegations and concluded that sponsors of local anti-Kennedy advertisements and handbills had no plans to harm the president.

Vietnam. Oliver Stone's film, "JFK," brought this theory into prominence. (*Figure 56*) His thesis, that Kennedy was killed to prevent American troops from pulling out of Vietnam, had some backing in *JFK and Vietnam,* a book based on the doctoral dissertation of John Newman. Newman argued that Kennedy did plan to pull out of Southeast Asia, but did not state that the plan may have led to the president's death. JFK planned the withdrawal of 1,000 troops before the end of 1963, but he was also on record that he did not "see the end of the tunnel" in the Vietnam conflict.

Figure 56
For his 1991 blockbuster conspiracy film, "JFK," Hollywood director Oliver Stone did a meticulous reconstruction of Dealey Plaza and filmed a detailed reenactment of the assassination on location. Here, a photo from the reenactment. The popular film fostered the growth of Vietnam theories about the assassination and led to a law requiring the declassification of government documents associated with the crime and its investigations. *David Woo, courtesy* The Dallas Morning News

Assassinations

Some nations have assassinated their leaders to effect change in policy, but the American political system of checks and balances assures fair governance, an orderly transfer of power is built into the system, and presidential candidates have traditionally chosen a running mate who shared their general political philosophy.

Still, John F. Kennedy was the fourth American president assassinated in office, and the eighth to be attacked since the first unsuccessful attempt against Andrew Jackson in 1835. Abraham Lincoln was shot in the head by John Wilkes Booth on April 14, 1865, while attending a performance of "Our American Cousin" at Ford's Theater in Washington, D.C. (*Figure 57*) He died the next morning. Booth was later killed trying to avoid capture, and seven conspirators were convicted of plotting the crime.

President James A. Garfield was shot in the back by Charles J. Guiteau in Washington, D.C., on July 2, 1881. Garfield died eleven weeks later. Guiteau was convicted and hanged. Leon Czolgosz shot President William McKinley during the Pan-American Exposition in Buffalo, N.Y., on September 6, 1901. McKinley died eight days later. Czolgosz was convicted and died in the electric chair. Oswald was the only presidential assassin to proclaim his innocence.

Assassination is a global occurrence. Abroad, political organizations have often been responsible for the death of a chief executive. In America the assassin has often been a lone individual. The death of President Lincoln is the only assassination that has consistently been ruled a conspiracy.

> *A hypnotist discovered in the early 1970's that a farm boy under her treatment was a reincarnation of Booth...she learned...that Booth had been paid by the Copperheads to kill Lincoln, that he had escaped to Europe, and died in 1875.*
> *The hypnotist found a significant parallel between the eighteen pages missing from Booth's diary and the eighteen minutes erased from President Nixon's famous tape.*
>
> •
>
> HISTORIAN WILLIAM HANCHETT
> The Lincoln Murder Conspiracies, *1986*

FIGURE 57
On April 14, 1865, actor John
Wilkes Booth shot President
Abraham Lincoln in the head
during a performance at Ford's
Theater in Washington, D.C.
Lincoln died the following day.
From Frank Leslie's Illustrated
News, *April 29, 1865, Sixth Floor
Museum Archives*

Americans have always reacted to presidential assassinations as a threat to the
stability of government. The office of the presidency symbolizes political leadership,
so assassination of the chief executive has traditionally been seen as a strike against
the government itself.

Each presidential murder has launched a period of increased public concern
about the major political issues of the day. Historically, such assassinations have not
generated major long-term changes in public policy. Instead, laws have been enacted
to strengthen the democratic system.

JOHN FITZGERALD KENNEDY

The Legacy

The assassination of John F. Kennedy had a profound effect on millions of people at home and abroad. Historians have found it difficult to assess Kennedy's presidency because it was cut short. Some of them assert that he accomplished little; others believe that he will ultimately rank among America's most significant leaders. Most concur that he deserves credit for "what might have been." (*Figure 58*)

Author Walter Lippman observed that "the final test of a leader is that he leaves behind him in other men the conviction and the will to carry on." Kennedy's death led to the passage of many of his major programs, partly through the efforts of his experienced successor, Lyndon B. Johnson. Johnson's pledge to "let us continue" was a commitment to carry on Kennedy's work. His own legacy is forever entwined with that of his predecessor.

In all, more than 200 bills, including over fifty of Kennedy's, passed the Congress under Johnson's initiative. Major accomplishments included the tax cut, the 1964 Civil Rights Act and other legislation, the Mass Transportation Act, Medicare, the Housing Act of 1965 and significant welfare programs.

FIGURE 58
Section of The Sixth Floor Museum examining the legacy of JFK.
Sixth Floor Museum Archives

To those who have the misfortune to die young, history assigns the role of inspirer.

•

HISTORIAN DANIEL J. BOORSTIN
U.S. News & World Report,
October 24, 1988

Legislatively, a constitutional amendment clarified presidential succession and the killing of a president or vice president was made a federal crime. Procedurally, presidential protection was enhanced and eventually expanded to include presidential candidates. On an emotional level the assassination of the president left a legacy of doubt among the people; a large majority of Americans still believe that there are unanswered questions about Kennedy's death.

President Kennedy's pledge to put a man on the moon was realized on July 21, 1969, when American astronauts Neil Armstrong and Edwin "Buzz" Aldrin walked on the lunar surface. The Peace Corps attracted more than 120,000 volunteers during its first quarter century of activity. John F. Kennedy shares the legacy of Vietnam with others. Escalation of the war after 1963 and direct U.S. involvement there alienated many Americans and led to widespread unrest. The invasion of Cambodia in 1970 galvanized anti-war opinion. American forces withdrew from Vietnam during the early 1970's and in 1975 the government fell to the communists.

Historians have debated whether Kennedy's death fostered national unrest during the later 1960's and 1970's. Certainly the assassination made John F. Kennedy a legend in the public mind. His popularity as a cultural hero is separate from the reasoned assessments of his political accomplishments. National public opinion polls taken since 1963 consistently name him the greatest American president in history. After his death, Kennedy's widow expressed concern that "his dreams" would be forgotten. But he remains a positive force in the collective memory, a memory that has passed to a new generation that never knew him. John F. Kennedy endures as a symbol of commitment and hope for effective change. These symbolic values may ultimately outlast the search for historical certainties.

JACQUELINE BOUVIER KENNEDY ONASSIS

Kennedy's widow provided the public with "Camelot" as the moniker to describe an era. Most concur that it ended only with her death from cancer in May 1994. After JFK's death, Jacqueline Kennedy tried to withdraw from the spotlight, but the media kept its glare on the beautiful widow and her two young children. Robert Kennedy was assassinated in June 1968, and in August of that year Jacqueline Kennedy married Greek shipping tycoon Aristotle Onassis. Subsequently, she spent several years jet-setting around the globe. Most observers contended that the marriage soured, and there were rumors of impending divorce when Onassis died in 1975. The former first lady settled permanently in the United States, mainly in an apartment in New York, where she entered the publishing world as a part-time editor, first at Viking and later at Doubleday.

Between 1975 and her death, Mrs. Onassis stubbornly maintained the right to privacy for herself and her children. She refused interviews and generally remained out of the public eye. In the area of historic preservation, she is credited with saving Grand Central Station in Manhattan and was occasionally a strong voice in other efforts to protect important historical structures. During the last decade of her life, she enjoyed the companionship of New York financier Maurice Tempelsman. Daughter Caroline, an attorney and author, married New York exhibit designer Edward Schlossberg in 1986. The couple has three children: Rose, Tatiana, and John. John F. Kennedy Jr. is also an attorney.

Jacqueline Kennedy Onassis's most impressive legacy was one of elegance and grace under pressure; her quiet strength and dignity during JFK's funeral endeared her to millions of people around the world. (*Figure 59*) The refurnishing of the White House remains another permanent tribute to her artistic talents, since subsequent administrations have made impressive additions to the collections in the "Nation's House." She is remembered as an outstanding mother who raised her children well, teaching them to deal responsibly with fame and wealth.

> *I think that my biggest achievement is that after going through a rather difficult time, I consider myself comparatively sane. I'm proud of that.*
>
> •
>
> JACQUELINE KENNEDY ONASSIS
> *ca. 1979*

FIGURE 59

A widowed Jacqueline Kennedy on the White House steps with her two children, prior to the congressional service in the rotunda of the Capitol on November 24, 1963. Mrs. Kennedy's courage during the weekend following the assassination was a powerful binding force for a suffering nation. It remains the strongest aspect of her legacy.

Courtesy AP/ Wide World Photos

There are no nationalities nor races in the ideal world of values...we held him as ours, and it is as ours that we have lost him.

•

EDITORIAL
Diario de Costa Rica, *San José*
November 24, 1963

FIGURE 60
The John F. Kennedy Center for the Performing Arts in Washington, D.C., is the permanent memorial in the nation's capital dedicated to the memory of the thirty-fifth president. *Courtesy Joan Marcus*

"No one we knew ever had a better sense of self," eulogized brother-in-law Senator Edward Kennedy at her funeral. Traumatized by the horror of Dallas and faced with raising two small children in the harsh light of global public attention, some would have faltered. Instead, she forged a satisfying life on her own terms and lived it well. She was buried beside John F. Kennedy and their two deceased infants at Arlington National Cemetery.

WORLD TRIBUTES

In the months and years that followed John F. Kennedy's death, nations and communities around the world created permanent memorials to his memory. The tributes ranged from towering Mount Kennedy in the Canadian Yukon to the simple Colegio John F. Kennedy on a dirt road in rural Argentina.

In the District of Columbia the American government named its new performing arts center for President Kennedy. (*Figure 60*) The John F. Kennedy Library and Museum opened its doors outside Boston in 1979 as a living memorial to the life and

political career of the thirty-fifth president. (*Figure 61*) Dealey Plaza National Historic Landmark was recognized in 1993 as a site that commemorates an important event in the history of the nation. Other commemorations are perhaps more humble, but all reflect a compelling admiration for the political and cultural legacy of JFK.

Hundreds of foreign streets bear John F. Kennedy's name, at least twenty-seven in Greece alone. Argentina named forty schools for JFK, and citizens of West Germany dedicated more than fifty memorials to the man who claimed "ich bin ein Berliner" in 1963. At home and abroad there are Kennedy airports, bridges, tunnels, civil and cultural centers, gardens, parks, statues and busts. Hundreds of nations issued commemorative stamps. The Kennedy half-dollar remains a popular collector's item among Americans.

What do these tributes mean? *Saturday Review* editor Norman Cousins reasoned that John Kennedy personified America's basic commitment "to advance the human cause on earth." He is remembered as a rich man committed to helping the poor, a white dedicated to the advancement of non-whites, an agent of positive change, a man who loved being president. The leader of Colombia observed to Kennedy in 1961, "The people believe you are on their side." The world tributes to Kennedy serve as lasting reminders of this powerful affection.

FIGURE 61

The John F. Kennedy Library and Museum outside Boston was designed by I.M. Pei and opened in 1979 as a memorial to the life of the slain leader.

Courtesy John F. Kennedy Library

History

Dealey Plaza
National Historic Landmark

The site where President John F. Kennedy was shot and killed was originally a part of the land grant deeded to Dallas founder John Neely Bryan during the early 1840's; the town's first businesses sprang up on the land now occupied by the plaza, which was constructed as a new vehicular gateway into the city between 1934 and 1940. (*Figure 62*) A part of the corn field that Bryan planted was discovered in 1988 during construction of The Sixth Floor Museum visitor center.

Prior to the 1930's, the Trinity River ran where the triple underpass now stands. Periodic flooding of the downtown area led the community to undertake a massive engineering project that moved the river a mile to the west. Stemmons Freeway was constructed on a part of the reclaimed river bottom; the creation of Dealey Plaza was the final phase of the project.

The plan for the park involved scooping out three acres of soil to create an underpass of three converging streets beneath a new railroad bridge connecting Union Terminal (1913) to the south with the rail yards (1880's and later) to the north. The bridge and basic engineering were completed between 1934 and 1935.

Garden structures in a modified Art Deco style were erected in the park between 1938 and 1940. The area was landscaped in 1940, with some additional plantings added by the city during the late 1950's. The initial beautification program was a cooperative effort of the City of Dallas, the Texas Highway Department and the Works Progress Administration, a federal New Deal program introduced by President Franklin D. Roosevelt during the Depression.

Dealey Plaza was officially named in 1935 for George Bannerman Dealey (1859-1946) publisher of *The Dallas Morning News* and a noted civic leader. The statue honoring Dealey, sculpted by Felix De Weldon in 1948, was placed on Houston Street in 1949. De Weldon is also remembered as the sculptor of the Iwo Jima Memorial near Washington, D.C.

Today we recognize the lasting place this site will forever have in our nation's history. It is hereby dedicated to the future generations of Americans with the hope that the legacy of John F. Kennedy will inspire them to reach for greatness in their own lives.

•

NELLIE CONNALLY
*Dedication of Dealey Plaza
National Historic Landmark
November 22, 1993*

All of the structures surrounding Dealey Plaza predate the Kennedy assassination, and all but two of them predate the construction of Dealey Plaza during the 1930's. The present landscape plan was in place in 1963, and all garden structures predate the assassination. Two highway signs on the north side of Elm were removed shortly after the shooting and replaced with the overhead sign at the corner of Elm and Houston. A third sign located in the grass north of Elm, closer to the triple underpass, was replaced during the late 1980's.

During the mid-1960's the city moved the lamp posts, originally in the sidewalks, six feet onto the grass and added more lighting on the south side of Elm and the north side of Commerce Street. A bronze tablet marking the presidential motorcade route was placed on Houston Street behind the obelisk at that time. Texas historical markers relating to the pioneer history of the site were placed near the colonnades during the 1970's, and the twin flagpoles were added in 1985.

In 1989 the National Park Service invited the Dallas County Historical Foundation to prepare an application to designate the assassination site as a National Historic Landmark. The application received tentative approval in 1991, and the Secretary of the Interior formally designated the landmark on October 12, 1993. Nellie Connally, widow of Governor John B. Connally, returned to Dealey Plaza on November 22, 1993 to dedicate the bronze landmark plaque before a crowd of 6,000 people. In her remarks she said: "Thirty years ago, fate brought me here as an unwilling player in the most unforgettable tragic drama of our times. Now, three decades later, we are gathered here not to look back with grief but to look forward with hope." (*Figure 63*)

The National Historic Landmark consists of Dealey Plaza, all surrounding buildings facing the park, the triple underpass bridge, and a

FIGURE 62
Dealey Plaza was built over the site of the original town of Dallas, founded during the early 1840's. Here, the park under construction in 1934-35. *Courtesy DeGolyer Library, Southern Methodist University, P294.3.192*

FIGURE 63
The Kennedy assassination site was designated a National Historic Landmark by the Secretary of the Interior in October 1993. Thousands of people attended ceremonies, shown here, on November 22, 1993. Former Texas First Lady Nellie Connally rededicated the site to history. *Ronald D. Rice, Sixth Floor Museum Archives*

portion of the rail yards west of the old Depository extending past the railroad switching tower. (*Figure 64*) Seven separate property owners cooperated in the designation. Dealey Plaza is a landmark district, one of two in Dallas and one of less than 100 in the United States. Texas claims a total of thirty-six National Historic Landmarks of the 1,800 nationwide. The bronze plaque is located in the grass north of Elm Street, near the spot where President Kennedy received his fatal wound.

FIGURE 64

Map showing the boundaries of Dealey Plaza National Historic Landmark. 1963 building names are used for the structures within the orange outline. The Sixth Floor Museum is housed in the former Texas School Book Depository Building. *Sixth Floor Museum Archives*

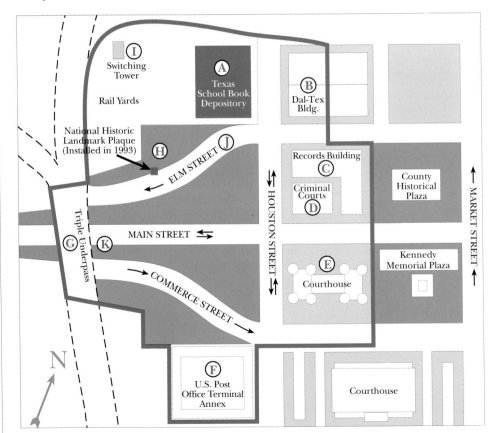

The best way to tour the assassination site is to review accounts provided by the people who actually witnessed the tragedy. Study the map in Figure 65, which shows the key areas in the site, the motorcade route and the location of some of the major witnesses. Their positions coincide with the time that the fatal shot struck President Kennedy in the head. Notice how their recollections varied about the sequence, timing and number of shots.

FIGURE 65
Map showing the motorcade route, in orange, and key witness locations in Dealey Plaza at the time of the fatal shot. *Map design courtesy R. B. Cutler. Research by Gary Mack.*

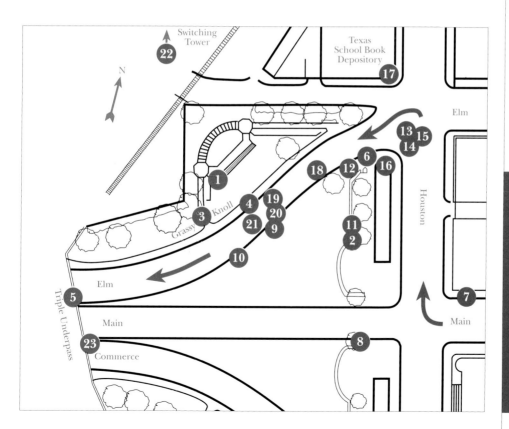

Please respect the structures and grounds and remain off the grass as much as possible by using sidewalks and pathways. The railroad bridge still carries trains; visitors are warned to walk on the bridge only at their own risk. It is illegal to remove materials or to deface the site.

The Witnesses

FIGURE 66

Pearl Harbor survivor Maj. Phil Willis snapped this picture just after he heard a shot ring out in Dealey Plaza. The limousine is shown passing in front of the Stemmons Freeway sign. Abraham Zapruder can be seen in the far background to the right and slightly above the level of the sign. The arrow indicates President Kennedy's location. *Phil Willis, Copyright 1964. Updated to Year 2039*

Although crowds had thinned out at the end of the parade, hundreds of people in Dealey Plaza either saw or heard the assassination of John F. Kennedy. For the first time in history, over two dozen of them recorded the killing of an American president on film. Most were amateur photographers who had come out to welcome President Kennedy and to take a photographic record of his visit to Dallas.

Seeing or hearing the president's violent death was traumatic, but some people believed that they were directly in the line of fire. Echo patterns in the plaza made it difficult for most witnesses to determine the origin or number of shots. They stated that they heard one to eight or more—many heard three—coming from various locations in Dealey Plaza. One distinct group thought shots came from the Texas School Book Depository; several people saw a rifle at an upper window at that location. Another, smaller group said shots came from the fenced area atop the garden on the north side of Elm Street, later named the grassy knoll. A few thought shots came from more than one direction.

The first major government investigation, the Warren Commission probe, used interviews from 190 witnesses; some people were not questioned, while others came forward later. Testimony taken immediately after the assassination was generally the most objective, since witnesses were not influenced by the massive news reportage that followed.

1. Abraham Zapruder: age 58, president of Jennifer Juniors, a dress company with offices in the Dal-Tex Building at 501 Elm Street. He heard two, possibly three shots, and filmed the entire assassination with an 8mm Bell & Howell camera. (*Figure 66*)

> *...then I started yelling "They killed him," they killed him, and...I was still shooting the pictures until he got under the underpass—I don't even know how I did it.*
>
> •
>
> ABRAHAM ZAPRUDER
> *Testimony taken July 22, 1964*

FIGURE 67
Dallas housewife Wilma Bond took
this picture after the limousine
had sped from the park. Here,
police race toward the scene. The
Newman family appears to the
north of Elm Street, still lying on
the grass. *Wilma Bond, courtesy the
estate of Wilma I. Bond*

2. Wilma I. Bond: housewife. She took nine clear 35mm color slides of the motor-cade on Houston Street and recorded activities on Elm Street immediately after the assassination. (*Figure 67*)

3. Emmett Joseph Hudson: age 56, Dallas Park Department grounds keeper. He heard three shots and thought they came from the grassy knoll.

4. William Eugene Newman: age 22, electrician. Newman heard two shots, and said that one seemed to have come from the hill behind him now known as the grassy knoll. The former military man and his wife fell to the ground, covering their young sons, after the fatal shot was fired.

*I thought the shot had come
from the garden directly behind
me, that was on an elevation
from where I was....*

•

WILLIAM E. NEWMAN
*Affidavit taken
November 22, 1963*

FIGURE 68
Orville Nix was standing a
considerable distance from the
assassination site when he filmed
Secret Service Agent Clint Hill
reaching for a toehold on the
limousine. Mrs. Kennedy is on
the trunk, reaching for a piece
of her husband's head. *Orville O.
Nix film copyright 1963,1990;
courtesy Gayle Nix Jackson*

*Then I heard another shot ring
out and Mrs. Kennedy jumped
up in the car and said,
"My God, he has been shot."*

•

MARY MOORMAN
Affidavit taken November 22, 1963

5. S.M. Holland: age 57, signal supervisor for Union Terminal Railroad. He heard four shots from two locations and saw "a puff of smoke" come from the trees at the fenced area atop the grassy knoll.

6. Hugh William Betzner: age 22. Betzner took three photographs and heard at least two shots.

7. Howard E. Elkins: Dallas County deputy sheriff. He heard three shots, which he thought came from the grassy knoll.

8. Orville Nix: General Services Administration employee. He took an 8mm film which recorded the final moments of the assassination. (*Figure 68*)

9. Mary Moorman: housewife. She took several black-and-white Polaroid photographs of the motorcade, including one that coincided closely with the fatal shot. She heard three or four shots. (*Figure 69*)

FIGURE 69
Mary Moorman, right, and Jean
Hill were standing close to the
limousine when the fatal shot was
fired. Moorman took the Polaroid
photo shown in Figure 21. Hill later
wrote a book about her experiences
as a witness to the shooting.
Dallas Times Herald *Collection,
Sixth Floor Museum Archives*

10. James "Ike" Altgens: age 44, Associated Press news photo editor and photographer. He took black and white photographs before, during and after the assassination in Dealey Plaza. Altgens said he heard at least three shots and believed they came from the Depository.(*Figure 72*)

11. Marie Muchmore. She took an 8mm film of the motorcade on Houston Street and also captured the final moments of the shooting.

12. Phillip L. Willis: age 46, retired Air Force major and Pearl Harbor survivor. The former state legislator took twenty-seven 35mm slides of the motorcade and Dealey Plaza before, during and after the assassination. Willis stated he heard three shots. (*Figure 66*)

13. Tom C. Dillard: age 49, chief photographer for *The Dallas Morning News.* Dillard believed shots came from the Depository and used two cameras to snap two photographs of the facade of the building immediately after the shooting. He heard three shots.

14. Malcolm O. Couch: age 25, theology student and television photographer. He heard three shots and saw a rifle barrel being drawn back into an upper window in the Depository building.

15. Robert Hill "Bob" Jackson: age 29, *Dallas Times Herald* photographer. Jackson heard three shots and saw a rifle protruding from the sixth floor corner window of the Depository.

I proceeded down the street....
I knew my little daughters were
running along beside the
presidential car, and I was
immediately concerned
about them....

•

PHIL WILLIS
Testimony taken July 22, 1964

There were five of us in the car. When we heard the first shot, the president had
already turned the corner [onto Elm] then we heard two more shots.

•

BOB JACKSON
Dallas Times Herald, *November 22, 1963*

16. Howard C. Brennan: age 44, steam fitter employed by Wallace and Beard Construction. Brennan saw a sniper fire from the sixth floor corner window of the Depository and heard two or possibly three shots. His description of the sniper was broadcast on police channels at 12:45 pm. (*Figure 70*)

> *...in the east end of the building and the second row of windows from the top I saw a man in the window....He was a white man in his early 30's, slender, nice looking, slender and would weigh about 165 to 175 pounds. He had on light colored clothing but definitely not a suit...and about...to a point...the president's back was in a line with the last window... I heard what I thought was a backfire....I then saw this man I have described in the window and he was taking aim with a high powered rifle....I was looking at the man in the window at the time of the last explosion.*
>
> •
>
> HOWARD BRENNAN
> *Affidavit taken November 22, 1963*

17. Harold Norman: age 25, employee at Texas School Book Depository. Norman viewed the parade from the fifth floor corner window of the warehouse and heard three shots fired from the window directly above him.

18. Ralph Yarborough: age 60, senator from Texas who rode in the vice president's limousine. He heard three shots fired from his right rear (direction of Depository).

19. Glenn Bennett: Secret Service agent who rode in the follow-up car behind JFK. He heard three shots and saw two shots hit the president from behind (direction of Depository).

20. Clinton J. Hill: Secret Service agent riding in the follow-up car. Hill heard two shots fired from behind him.

21. John B. Connally: age 46, governor of Texas. He heard two shots but believed there were three, and that he was hit by a shot fired after President Kennedy was wounded in the back.

22. Lee Bowers: age 36, railroad switchman in the railroad switching tower roughly ninety yards north of the grassy knoll. Bowers said he heard three shots and saw unfamiliar automobiles in the rail yards shortly before the assassination. He also saw two men standing behind the picket fence at the grassy knoll during the shooting.

23. James Thomas Tague: age 27, car salesman for Cedar Springs Dodge. Tague heard three shots and was wounded on the cheek during the shooting by an unlocated bullet fragment that ricocheted off the curb nearby.

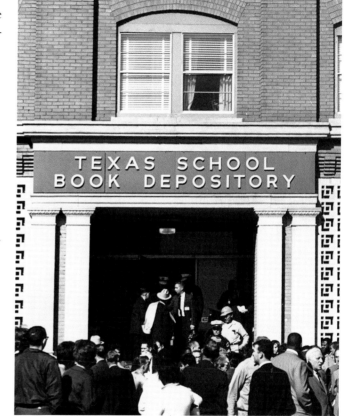

FIGURE 70
Assassination witness Howard Brennan, seen in the distance on the
steps of the Depository wearing a hard hat, saw a sniper fire on
the motorcade from the sixth floor of the Depository.
Brennan offered a description to police shortly after the shooting.
©*Jim Murray Film - all rights reserved*

"I recall something sting [sic] me on the face while I was standing down there."

•

JAMES TAGUE
Testimony taken July 23, 1964

Description of the Site

See Figure 64 on page 72 for a larger reproduction of this map.

or more than a decade after 1963, the assassination site was an active criminal investigative scene. Governmental agencies staged three reenactments of the shooting there between 1963 and 1978. Film makers have also used the layout for partial reenactments over the years, and amateur assassination researchers are regular visitors in the area.

Since many researchers have argued that snipers fired on the motorcade from buildings other than the Depository, an overview of the key structures and locations at the site and their relationship to the assassination is offered here. This description provides the names of buildings as they were used in 1963, followed by the modern name. (*Figure 64*)

A. Texas School Book Depository (built 1901 by Southern Rock Island Plow Company of Illinois; now Dallas County Administration Building), 411 Elm Street.

This seven-story, 80,000 square-foot brick warehouse was constructed to store and showcase farming equipment. It replaced an 1898 warehouse there which burned in 1901. In 1909 the plow company sold the structure, and in 1939 it passed into the hands of the Byrd family of Dallas, which used it as a rental property. The building is in the modified classical warehouse style, with arched windows and brick pilasters.

At the time of the assassination the warehouse was rented to the Texas School Book Depository Company, a private business that stored and shipped text books to Texas schools. Several book publishers' representatives also kept offices there. (*Figure 71*)

The major official investigations into the assassination agreed that all shots that hit the occupants of the presidential limousine were fired from the sixth floor, southeast corner window of the Depository. Several witnesses to the shooting saw a rifle there, and immediately after the shooting investigators found evidence in that location. Lee Harvey Oswald, the alleged assassin, was employed as an order clerk at the Depository.

In 1970 the Depository Company moved to another Dallas location and the structure was offered for sale. Between 1970 and 1972 it was in the hands of a promoter from Nashville, Tennessee, who defaulted on his loan in the latter year. An arsonist tried to burn down the building in 1972 without success; another arson fire in 1984 damaged a small part of the basement. Dallas County purchased the decayed warehouse late in 1977 and began a long-term renovation of parts of the building to convert it into a new seat of administrative government. The sixth floor was sealed to assure its preservation.

Some elements of the building that were present in 1963 had to be removed during the renovation; all were either documented in detail or physically preserved as a part of the collections of The Sixth Floor Museum. They include the large Hertz advertising sign that was on top of the building, the roof parapet, the cinder-block screens from the first floor windows, an ell addition on the west side, the loading dock from the north side, the Houston Street fire escape, and the second floor lunchroom, where Oswald was detained about two minutes after the shooting.

The sixth floor of the building was restored in 1988 and adapted into The Sixth Floor Museum, which opened to the public in 1989. The museum, accessible from a separate visitor center on the north side of the old Depository, is open daily except December 25. Admission fees support museum and research center operations, preservation of collections and publication programs. The museum is operated by the private non-profit Dallas County Historical Foundation, which was incorporated in 1983.

B. Dal-Tex Building (built 1902, by Kingman-Texas Implements Company; annex added, 1904; now 501 Elm Place, Hubbell and Greene, Dallas, architects), 501 Elm Street.

Assassination witness Abraham Zapruder and several other dress manufacturers maintained offices in this building in 1963, hence the name, Dallas Textile or Dal-Tex Building. Investigators searched the warehouse after the shooting, but found no physical evidence associated with the murder of the president. One man was detained for questioning but released. Some assassination researchers believe that a sniper could have fired on the motorcade from the roof, or from a window on the second or fourth floor of this structure. (*Figure 72*) The Houston Street fire escape, present in 1963, was removed; window awnings and the Houston Street entrance are later additions. [*private, not open for tours*]

FIGURE 71
View of the Texas School Book Depository taken from Houston Street on November 22, 1963. *Sixth Floor Museum Archives*

FIGURE 72
Photo taken by witness James "Ike" Altgens shortly after the president received his back wound. The Dal-Tex building appears in the background. Some researchers have used enhancement techniques, searching for a sniper near the fire escape shown here. *James Altgens, courtesy AP/Wide World Photos*

C. Dallas County Records Building Annex (built 1955, Smith, Worden, Nelson & Corgan, Dallas, architects), 500 Elm Street

No formal search of the annex was performed following the shooting. Theorists have suggested that a sniper might have been able to fire at the motorcade from the roof of this building. Neither suspects nor evidence has been located to support this hypothesis. The exterior retains its 1963 appearance. [*not open for tours*]

D. Dallas County Criminal Courts Building (built 1913-15, now Old Criminal Courts Building, A. H. Overbeck, architect), 500 Main Street.

In 1963 the structure housed the Dallas County Sheriff's Department and a part of the county jail system. Sheriff's deputies took witness affidavits in this building immediately after the shooting. Lee Harvey Oswald was being transferred to the jail here when he was gunned down by Jack Ruby on November 24, 1963. Jack Ruby was incarcerated here, and his trial was held in one of the courtrooms in the building. The exterior was renovated during the 1980's but retains its 1963 appearance. This building has never been seriously named as a potential assassin location. [*not open for tours*]

E. Dallas County Courthouse (built 1892, now Old Red Courthouse, M.A. Orlopp, Little Rock, principal architect), Houston and Commerce Streets.

The Old Red Courthouse, a handsome Victorian building in the Romanesque Revival style, is the fifth courthouse erected on the one square block of land donated for this purpose by Dallas founder John Neely Bryan in 1850. At the time of the assassination it was still the main county courthouse; the "new" courthouse building on Commerce Street was then under construction. One witness, Patsy Paschall, filmed part of the motorcade and scenes after the shooting from this building. With the exception of the roof, which was restored in 1987, the Old Red retains its 1963 exterior appearance. Old Red has not been regarded as a potential sniper location. [*closed for restoration*]

F. United States Post Office Terminal Annex (built 1937, now Federal Building, Lang & Witchell, Dallas, architects), Southwest corner of Houston and Commerce Streets.

Lee Harvey Oswald rented a post office box in this building, using the alias A. J. Hidell, and used it to order the rifle used in the assassination. The main post office lobby, located on Houston Street, contains handsome murals—"Air Mail Over Texas" and "Pioneer Homebuilders"—painted in 1940 by noted Texas artist Peter Hurd. The lobby is open for viewing during normal business hours. Admission is free. Renovated by the General Services Administration during the 1980's, the exterior retains its historic appearance. One witness observed the motorcade, the assassination and its immediate aftermath from the roof of this building.

G. Triple Underpass and Bridge (built 1934-35)
   Although the bridge was closed to pedestrians during the motorcade, there were Dallas policemen and several railroad employees on the span when the shots were fired. Many of them observed the assassination.

H. The Grassy Knoll/MKT Railroad Yards (Knoll built 1934-40; rail yards, 1880's and later. The yards are now Union Pacific Rail Yards and a Dallas Area Rapid Transit light rail thoroughfare)
   The grassy knoll is the hillock that rises from the north side of Elm Street to the edge of the picket fence separating Dealey Plaza from the Missouri, Kansas & Texas railroad yards. At the time of the assassination, the rail yards contained five curved spurs, six north-south tracks converging into four at the triple underpass bridge, a switching tower, unpaved parking for railroad and Depository employees, and a one-story shed. The area nearest the picket fence was used for parking. Take a look at the 1963 Squire Haskins aerial photograph of the area, illustrated at the front of this guide book; it shows the historic features clearly.
   The railroad demolished the shed in 1989 and replaced it with a small brick building. Some of the spurs were taken out during the late 1970's, and the remainder of the track was removed in 1987-90, when the area was paved for parking. The pickets in the fence have suffered from souvenir hunters. The DART light rail line was added in 1993-1995.
   Some witnesses said that shots came from this area, but investigators found only

cigarette butts and foot prints behind the fence. Others who ran into the rail yards after the assassination said they were stopped there by Secret Service agents, although the government concluded that none were assigned to that location.

The House Select Committee used scientific acoustical analysis for its investigation in 1976-78, and concluded that a sniper, located behind the picket fence, fired on the motorcade and missed. The analysis placed the sniper about eight feet west of the corner of the fence near the steps. This data was instrumental in leading the committee to conclude that President Kennedy had been killed as a result of a conspiracy. The acoustic analysis was disputed in 1982 by another government-sponsored committee, thus undermining the House panel's ruling for a conspiracy. The area remains the most controversial part of the assassination site.

I. Switching Tower (built 1916 by MKT Railroad, now owned by Dallas Area Rapid Transit)

The old railroad switching tower is still used for rail operations; it retains much of its 1963 exterior appearance. Railroad Switchman Lee Bowers was in the tower at the time of the shooting and testified that he saw strange cars in the parking lot prior to the shooting and noticed two men standing at the edge of the yards at the picket fence when the assassination took place.

J. Elm Street (named by Dallas founder John Neely Bryan in 1844, present street laid out in 1934-35)

The entire assassination took place while the presidential limousine was traveling down Elm Street in the middle lane at an average speed of 11 mph. The shooting occurred at a distance roughly 166 feet to 231 feet from the Houston Street/Elm Street intersection. To gain an easier understanding of the sequence of shots, find the white lane dividers on the street. There are pairs of stripes separating the street into three lanes. Start with the pair of stripes nearest the corner of Elm and Houston Streets.

The limousine made the 120-degree turn from Houston onto Elm Street at 12:30 pm, passing directly beneath the facade of the Texas School Book Depository. The Warren Commission ruled in 1964 that all shots were fired from the southeast corner window of the sixth floor of the Depository. The first shot to hit the occupants of the limousine, said the commission, was fired at Zapruder frames 210-224, at which time the president was between the third and fourth set of stripes. The commission was uncertain about the second shot, and noted that it might have been the fatal shot, at Zapruder frame 313, when the president's head was located at the start of the sixth stripe. The commission said that it was possible, but unlikely, that another shot was fired from the Depository after Zapruder frame 313.

According to the House Select Committee, the first shot was fired at the president from the sixth floor corner window at Zapruder frames 158-161. Using the president's head as a location point, JFK was located midway into the second pair of stripes. This shot supposedly missed the occupants of the limousine. The House said that the second shot was fired from the Depository at Zapruder frames 188-191, placing the president in the middle of the third set of stripes. This shot, said the committee, hit the president in the back, exited his neck, and then traveled into Governor Connally's back, breaking a rib, puncturing his lung, exiting his chest, fracturing his wrist, and finally lodging in his thigh.

The House placed the grassy knoll shot, which it said missed, at Zapruder frame 295; at that time the president was located midway between the fifth and sixth set of stripes. The fatal shot, said the House, was fired from the Depository and hit the president at Zapruder frame 313, when JFK was located at the beginning of the sixth stripe.

The National Historic Landmark bronze plaque is located in the grass on the north side of Elm Street in the general area where the fatal shot struck the president. A part of President Kennedy's skull was retrieved from the south side of Elm Street one day after the shooting. Elm Street has been repaved over the years.

K. Curbstone with Mark (Approach with caution; heavy traffic)

Car salesman James Tague got stuck in traffic in Dealey Plaza during the motorcade, and stepped out of his car on Commerce Street for a peek at the president and first lady. When he heard shots, he ducked behind a pillar supporting the triple underpass bridge. After the limousine left the park, Tague went to a deputy sheriff to report his recollections of the event, and was told that he had blood on his cheek.

He and investigators found a mark on the curb on the south side of Main Street, which was photographed by *Dallas Morning News* photographer Tom Dillard the following day. (*Figure 73*) The FBI finally removed the curbing in August 1964, and took it to Washington for analysis. The mark, said the FBI, was caused by a bullet fragment, which presumably ricocheted off the concrete and struck Tague in the cheek. The actual location of the mark was 23 feet 4 inches east of the triple underpass on the south side of Main Street. The piece of curbing remains in the National Archives in Washington, D.C.

FIGURE 73

Tom C. Dillard, chief photographer for *The Dallas Morning News,* took this picture of the mark on the curb on Main Street on November 23, 1963. The FBI later ruled that the mark was caused by a bullet fragment. *Tom C. Dillard, Sixth Floor Museum Archives*

Later during the afternoon of November 23, 1963 [Tom] Dillard ...took a picture of a mark on the curb on the south side of Main Street about twenty feet east of the triple underpass.

•

FBI REPORT
Warren Commission Volume 21
July 17, 1964

FIGURE 74

The John F. Kennedy Memorial, located one block east of the assassination site, was a gift of the citizens of Dallas county in memory of JFK. The cenotaph, or open tomb, was designed by noted American architect Philip Johnson as his first memorial commission. The memorial was dedicated in 1970. *Courtesy Robert Staples*

DALLAS COUNTY HISTORICAL PLAZA

Located one block east of the assassination site between Elm and Main Streets, Historical Plaza contains Dallas' oldest pioneer log cabin, ca. 1850, and a terrazzo map of the community's earliest settlements. The plaza was created after the assassination. At the time of the shooting the log cabin was located just south of the Old Red Courthouse facing Houston Street, having been moved there from another location in 1936.

JOHN F. KENNEDY MEMORIAL PLAZA

Located one block east of Dealey Plaza between Main and Commerce Streets, the plaza and memorial were a gift of the people of Dallas county in memory of President John F. Kennedy. (*Figure 74*) The memorial is a cenotaph, or open tomb, designed by noted American architect Philip Johnson. Jacqueline Kennedy was consulted on the design, which was Johnson's first memorial commission. Planning for construction of the memorial began in 1964; the one square block of land was donated by Dallas County. Construction of an underground parking garage delayed completion of the memorial, which was officially dedicated in 1970.

For many years, the community held annual observances honoring President Kennedy at the memorial on November 22, a practice that was discontinued in 1986 at the request of the Kennedy family, who asked that all services for JFK be held on May 29, the anniversary of his birth.

WEST END ENTERTAINMENT DISTRICT

The fifty-five acre West End Historic District, centered north and east of the assassination site, is one of Dallas's liveliest areas for entertainment and dining. (*Figure 75*) Over six million visitors per year attend musical concerts, festivals and other activities in the West End, which was listed on the National Register of Historic Places in 1978 as an important surviving warehouse district from the 1900-1920 era. The district includes more than fifty restaurants, a festival marketplace, an aquarium and a movie theater. The visitor's booth in the marketplace offers area maps and information about special events. The main entrance into the district is on Market Street, two blocks east of Dealey Plaza off Elm Street.

Nearby Services and Attractions

FIGURE 75
The West End Historic District, just north and east of Dealey Plaza, is one of the city's most popular entertainment areas. It attracts more than six million visitors per year. *Courtesy West End Association*

Suggestions for Further Reading

Millions of pages have been printed about John F. Kennedy's life, millions more about his death. The literature on the assassination is both vast and confusing to the average reader. The following books are offered, because most of them are readily available at most libraries; they will provide an overview of the assassination and some insights into the nature of the debate about who was responsible for the death of John F. Kennedy. The museum and the author do not attest to the accuracy of the information in any of these volumes, and their inclusion is not an endorsement of any particular viewpoint.

GOVERNMENT PUBLICATIONS

Unless noted otherwise, all publications were issued by the United States Government Printing Office, Washington, D.C.

Kennedy, John F. *Public Papers of the Presidents of the United States.* 1962-1964.
National Research Council. *Report of the Committee on Ballistic Acoustics.* 1982.
Panel Review of Photographs, X-ray Films, Documents and Other Evidence Pertaining to the Fatal Wounding Of President John F. Kennedy on November 22, 1963 in Dallas, Texas. 1968. [Clark Panel]
U. S. Commission on CIA Activities Within the United States. *Report to the President.* 1975. New York: Manor Books, 1976. [Rockefeller Commission]
U. S. House of Representatives, Select Committee on Assassinations. *Report* and 12 volumes of Hearings and Exhibits, 1979. *Report.* Bantam Edition, 1979. [House Select Committee]
U. S. President's Commission on the Assassination of President John F. Kennedy. *Report* and 26 volumes of Hearings and Exhibits, 1964. *Report.* Bantam Edition, 1964; St. Martin's Press Edition, 1993. [Warren Commission]
U.S. Senate Select Committee to Study Governmental Operations with Respect to Intelligence Agencies. *Alleged Assassination Plots Involving Foreign Leaders: Interim Report.* 1975. [Church Committee]
——*Investigation of the Assassination of President John F. Kennedy, Book V., Final Report.* 1976.

BOOKS AND ARTICLES

Associated Press. *The Torch is Passed....* New York: Associated Press, 1963.
Belin, David W. *November 22, 1963: You Are the Jury.* New York: Quadrangle, 1973.
——*Final Disclosure: The Truth About the Assassination of President Kennedy.* New York: Scribner, 1988.
Bell, J. Bowyer. *Assassin!* New York: St. Martin's Press, 1979.
Blakey, G. Robert, and Richard N. Billings. *The Plot to Kill the President.* New York: Times Books, 1981.
Boorstin, Daniel. "JFK His Vision: Now and Then." *U.S. News & World Report.* October 24, 1988.
Brener, Milton E. *The Garrison Case: A Study in the Abuse of Power.* New York: Clarkson N. Potter, 1969.
Brennan, Howard, with J. Edward Cherryholmes. *Eyewitness to History.* Waco, Texas: Texian Press, 1987.
Brown, Thomas. *JFK: History of an Image.* Bloomington, Indiana: Indiana University Press, 1988.
Callahan, Bob. *Who Shot JFK?* New York: Simon & Schuster, 1993.
Canfield, Michael, and Alan J. Weberman. *Coup d'Etat in America: The CIA and the Assassination of John F. Kennedy.* New York: Third Press, 1975.
Curry, Jesse. *JFK Assassination File.* Dallas: American Poster and Printing Company, 1969.
The Dallas Morning News. November 22: The Day Remembered. Dallas: Taylor Publishing Company, 1990.
Davis, John H. *The Kennedys: Dynasty and Disaster.* New York: McGraw-Hill, 1984.

——*Mafia Kingfish: Carlos Marcello and the Assassination of John F. Kennedy.* New York: Times Books, 1980.

Edelman, Murray, and Rita James Simon. "Presidential Assassinations: Their Meaning and Impact on Society." *Ethics.* Vol. 79, No. 3 (April 1969).

Epstein, Edward Jay. *Inquest: The Warren Commission and the Establishment of the Truth.* New York: Bantam, 1966; Viking, 1966.

Fonzi, Gaeton. *The Last Investigation.* New York: Thunder Mouth Press, 1993.

Ford, Gerald R., and John R. Stiles. *Portrait of the Assassin.* New York: Simon & Schuster, 1965.

Fox, Sylvan. *The Unanswered Questions About President Kennedy's Assassination.* New York: Award Books, 1975.

Frewin, Anthony. *The Assassination of John F. Kennedy: An Annotated Film, TV, and Videography.* Westport, CT: Greenwood Press, 1993.

Garrison, Jim. *On the Trail of the Assassins: My Investigation and Prosecution of the Murder of President Kennedy.* New York: Sheridan Square Press, 1988.

Groden, Robert. *The Killing of a President.* New York: Viking Penguin, 1993.

——and Harrison Livingston. *High Treason: The Assassination of John F. Kennedy.* Baltimore: Conservatory Press, 1989.

Guth, LeLoyd J., and David R. Wrone. *The Assassination of John F. Kennedy: A Comprehensive Historical and Legal Bibliography.* Westport, CT: Greenwood Press, 1980.

Hamilton, Nigel. *JFK: Reckless Youth.* New York: Random House, 1992.

Hanchett, William. *The Lincoln Murder Conspiracies.* Urbana and Chicago: University of Illinois Press, 1986.

Hennelly, Robert, and Jerry Policoff. "JFK: How the Media Assassinated the Real Story." *The Village Voice.* March 31, 1992.

Heymann, David C. *A Woman Named Jackie.* New York: Lyle Stewart/Carrol Communications, 1989.

Hunt, Conover. *The Sixth Floor: John F. Kennedy and the Memory of a Nation.* Dallas: Dallas County Historical Foundation, 1989.

Hurt, Henry. *Reasonable Doubt.* New York: Holt, Rinehart and Winston, 1985.

Johnson, Lyndon Baines. *The Vantage Point.* New York: Popular Press, 1971.

Kantor, Seth. *Who Was Jack Ruby?* Costa Mesa, CA: Everest House Press, 1978.

Kurtz, Michael. *Crime of the Century: The Kennedy Assassination From a Historian's Perspective.* Knoxville, TN: The University of Tennessee Press, 1982.

Lane, Mark. *Rush to Judgment.* New York: Holt, Rinehart and Winston, 1966.

Lattimer, John K., M.D. *Kennedy and Lincoln: Medical and Ballistic Comparisons of Their Assassinations.* San Diego, CA: Harcourt Brace Jovanovich, 1980.

Lasch, Christopher. "The Life of Kennedy's Death." *Harper's.* October, 1983.

Lerner, Max. "The World Impact." *New Statesman.* December 23, 1963

Life Articles:

   Assassination Issue. November 29, 1963.

   Connally, John B. "Why Kennedy Went to Texas. "November 24, 1967.

   John F. Kennedy Memorial Edition. December 6, 1963.

   "A Matter of Reasonable Doubt." November 25, 1966.

   "Remembering Jackie: A Life in Pictures." June, 1994.

Lifton, David. *Best Evidence: Disguise and Deception in the Assassination of John F. Kennedy.* New York: Carol & Graf, 1988.

Linenthal, Edward Tabor. *Sacred Ground.* Urbana and Chicago: University of Illinois Press, 1991.

Loftus, Elizabeth. *Eyewitness Testimony.* Cambridge, MA: Harvard University Press, 1979.

Lowe, Jacques. *Kennedy: A Time Remembered.* New York: Quartet Books, 1983.

Lowenthal, David. *The Past is a Foreign Country.* Cambridge, England: Cambridge University Press, 1985.

Manchester, William. *The Death of a President.* New York: Harper & Row, 1967.

Marrs, Jim. *Crossfire: The Plot That Killed Kennedy.* New York: Carol & Graf, 1989.

Meagher, Sylvia, and Gary Owens. *Master Index to the J.F.K. Assassination.* Metuchen, NJ and London: Scarecrow Press, 1980.

——. *Accessories After the Fact: The Warren Commission, the Authorities and the Report.* New York: Vantage, 1976.

Moore, Jim. *Conspiracy of One.* Fort Worth: The Summit Group, 1990.

Newman, John M. *JFK and Vietnam: Deception, Intrigue and Struggle for Power.* New York: Warner Books, 1992.

Noonan, Peggy. "America's First Lady." *Time.* May 30, 1994.

O'Donnell, Kenneth, and Dave Powers. *Johnny We Hardly Knew Ye: Memories of John Fitzgerald Kennedy.* New York: Little Brown, 1972.

Panter-Downs, Mollie. "Letter From London." *The New Yorker.* December 7, 1963.

Parker, Edwin B., and Bradley S. Greenberg, eds. *The Kennedy Assassination and the American Public: Social Communications in Crisis.* Stanford, CA: Stanford University Press, 1965.

Parmet, Herbert. *The Struggles of John F. Kennedy.* New York: Dial Press, 1980.

——*JFK: The Presidency of John F. Kennedy.* New York: Dial Press, 1983.

Payne, Darwin. *The Press Corps and the Kennedy Assassination.* Journalism Monographs. Association for Education in Journalism, 1989.

Pennebaker, James. *Opening Up: The Healing Power of Confiding in Others.* New York: William Morrow and Company, Inc., 1990.

Popkin, Richard. *The Second Oswald.* New York: Avon, 1966.

Posner, Gerald. *Case Closed.* New York: Random House, 1993.

Rice, Gerald T. *The Bold Experiment: JFK's Peace Corps.* Notre Dame, Indiana: University of Notre Dame Press, 1985.

Russell, John. "Portrait of a Friendship." *Time.* May 30, 1994.

Robertson, James O. *American Myth American Reality.* New York: Hill & Wang, 1980.

Salinger, Pierre. *With Kennedy.* New York: Doubleday, 1966.

Schachtman, Tom. *Decade of Shocks: From Dallas to Watergate 1963-1975.* New York: Poseidon, 1983.

Scheim, David E. *Contract on America: The Mafia Murders of John and Robert Kennedy.* Lakewood, CO: Argyle Press, 1983.

Schlesinger, Arthur M., Jr. *A Thousand Days: John F. Kennedy in the White House.* Boston: Houghton Mifflin, 1965.

Sorensen, Theodore C. *Kennedy.* New York: Harper & Row, 1965.

Stone, Oliver, and Zachary Sklar with Jane Rusconi. *JFK The Book of the Film.* Santa Barbara, CA: Applause Books, 1992.

Summers, Anthony. *Conspiracy.* New York: Paragon, 1991.

Thompson, Josiah. *Six Seconds in Dallas.* New York: Bernard Geis Associates, 1967; Berkley, 1976.

Trellin, Calvin. "The Buffs." *New Yorker.* June 10, 1967.

United Press International and *American Heritage* Magazine. *Four Days.* New York: UPI and *American Heritage,* 1964.

Van Der Karr, Richard K. "How Dallas Stations Covered Kennedy Shooting." *Journalism Quarterly.* Autumn 1965.

The Way We Were: 1963, The Year Kennedy was Shot. New York: Carrol & Graf, 1983.

Wecht, Cyril H., M.D. "JFK Revisited." *Journal of the American Medical Association.* Vol. 269, No. 12 (March 24/31, 1993).

Weinstein, Edwin A., and Olga G. Lyerly. "Symbolic Aspects of Presidential Assassination." *Psychiatry.* Vol. 32, No. 1 (February 1969).

Weisberg, Harold. *Whitewash.* New York: Dell, 1966.

——. *Whitewash II: The FBI Secret Service Cover Up.* New York: Dell, 1966/67.

White, Theodore. *America in Search of Itself: The Making of a President, 1956-1980.* New York: Harper & Row, 1982.

"A World Listened and Watched." *Broadcasting.* December 2, 1963.

Wright, Lawrence. *In the New World: Growing Up With America.* New York: Knopf, 1988.

Zelizer, Barbie. *Covering the Body: The Kennedy Assassination, the Media, and the Shaping of Collective Memory.* Chicago and London: University of Chicago Press, 1992.

Special thanks to those individuals and institutions who shared their collections and expertise for this publication: William Allen, Tony Auth, James Altgens, AP/Wide World Photos, James D. Baldwin, William Beal, Bettmann Archives, Jim Borgman, Camera Press, R. B. Cutler, *The Dallas Morning News*, Tom Dawson, DeGolyer Library/ Southern Methodist University, Tom C. Dillard, Virginia Fain, Glenda Haskins, Darryl Heikes, Bob Jackson, Gayle Nix Jackson, Lyndon Baines Johnson Library, John F. Kennedy Library, King Features Syndicate, Mary Ann Moorman Krahmer, Robert Knudsen, Jerry Marcus, Joan Marcus, James MacCammon, Jim Murray, National Archives, Pat Oliphant, Andy Reisberg, Retna Ltd., Ronald D. Rice, Staples & Charles, Ltd., Cecil W. Stoughton, Bret St. Clair, Robert Staples, Howard Upchurch, Al Volkland, Tina Wanner, West End Association, Marilyn Willis, Bill Winfrey and David Woo.

Thanks to those involved in the designation of the Dealey Plaza National Historic Landmark: Task Force Chairman Meg Read, Mrs. Reuben H. Adams, Pedro Aguirre, Jim Anderson, Edward Bearss, Walter S. Blake, Michelle Bleiberg, Roy Bode, Marvin Bullard, Larry Burnside, Jim Charleton, Mrs. John Cheney, Allen Clemson, Michael H. Collins, John E. Cook, Jeff Cotner, John Crain, Will Craven, DART, City of Dallas, Levi Davis, Yvonne Davis, David Dunnigan, Paul Dyer, City of Fort Worth, Judith Garrett, A.C. Gonzales, Robert J. Hays, Walter Herring, Conover Hunt, H.B. "Chip" Johnson, Doug Kowalski, Stan Levenson, Glenn Linden, Richard Lyon, Neil Mangum, Suzanne Martin, Jackie McElhaney, William A. McKenzie, Ralph Mendez, Norma Minnis, National Park Service, Trudy O'Reilly, Jodie Pogue, Nancy Powell, Read-Poland, Andrew Robinson, Wanda J. Schafer, Dick Sellars, Karla Silva, Kelly Snook, Gene Sparks, S.S. Sparks, Jr., Jim Steeley, Michael Steindorf, Andrew Stern, Annette Strauss, Sherry Tupper, the United States Government, John Ware and Jeff West.

Current and former members of the Dallas County Commissioners Court: Paul Bass, Mike Cantrell, Frank Crowley, David G. Fox, Lee F. Jackson, Jim Jackson, Nancy Judy, Kenneth A. Mayfield, Roy Orr, David Pickett, John Wiley Price, Chris V. Semos, Jim Tyson, Garry Weber and John Whittington.

Acknowledgments

Current and former members of the Board of Trustees of the Dallas County Historical Foundation: Mrs. Reuben H. Adams, Betty Agee, Pedro Aguirre, Walter S. Blake, Lillian M. Bradshaw, Mrs. Clifton Caldwell, Robert L. Canavan, Jr. , Mrs. John Cheney, Michael H. Collins, William E. Collins, W. E. Cooper, John Crain, Joe Dealey, Sr., Victor J. Elmore, Ruben E. Esquivel, Jack Evans, David G. Fox, Fred Harrington, Jess Hay, Mrs. C.H. Jankowski, Rex Jobe, Dr. Glenn Linden, William A. McKenzie, Samuel A. Moreno, Boone Powell, Sr., Mrs. Robert Power, Meg Read, Major General (Ret.) Hugh G. Robinson, Phillip S. Shinoda, Dr. Thomas Smith, Gene Sparks, Andrew Stern, Annette Strauss, Sherry Tupper, Mrs. Ben Weber, and Albert E. Whitting.

Staff of The Sixth Floor Museum involved with this publication:
Jeff West, Executive Director
Janice Babineaux, Deputy Director of Operations
Marian Ann Montgomery, Director of Interpretation
Gary Mack, Archivist
all other staff as of July 1, 1995: Kenneth Akbar, John Armour, James Bagby, Donnell Banks, Kevin Berry, Valente Briones, Alan Chavero, Sonia Cervantes, Larissa Church, Stacy Conaway, Tina Garcia, Ronald Gonzales, Pedro Gonzalez, Carol Hernandez, Sue Hilty, Gary Karwacki, David Kilbourn, Bertrand Lamb, Ruthie Lawson, Richard Oats, Robert Porter, Cheryl Price, Katrina Rhaney, Nathalie Ryan, Dora Soto, Michael Splendoria, Bret St.Clair, Timothy Tazelaar, Aaron Thomas, Raymond Weaver, Karen Wiley and Sanford Williams.